Farewell, my Lovely

Farewell, my Lovely

short tails and tributes
to Brains the MagnifiCat
and other much-loved, departed pets

Compiled by Susie Cornfield

Illustrations by Sara Rapoport

Farewell, my Lovely
Published in 2006 by Garret Books
ISBN 0 9552279 1 7; 978 0 9552279 1 2

The publisher thanks for their help Miriam Valencia at the Poetry Library, Royal Festival Hall; and Lisa Dowdeswell and Jo Hodder at The Society of Authors.

Garret Books Ltd, Company Registration Number: 05647052
Registered address: 4 Masons Avenue, Croydon, Surrey CR0 9XS
www.garretbooks.com

A CIP catalogue record for this book is available from the British Library.

Designed and typeset by Caroline and Roger Hillier, The Old Chapel Graphic Design
www.theoldchapelivinghoe.com
Copy Editor: Ros Lavine
Publishing assistant: Isobel Rapoport

Printed and bound in Great Britain by Biddles Ltd, King's Lynn, Norfolk.

In loving memory of
my father, Roy Cooper, and Bob,
Dilys Powell and Spike,
and
Sylvia Myers, the swan of Liverpool

Farewell, my Lovely is a tribute to
Brains the MagnifiCat,
and Hercules, Brimble, Cinnamon,
Mabel, Daisy, Jack, Barley, Fortnum,
Hero, Rover, Jeremy, Tommy, Sparky,
Teddy, Calypso Dancer, Gurami,
Sandy, Henrietta, Sweep, Monty,
Victor, Rosie, Monty, Powerjaws,
George, Baby, Zak, Pushkin and Bob.
With profound thanks to the humans who
shared their stories with me, including
those whose tales aren't in this book.

Contents

Foreword

I still remember the last day in the life of Finnegan, the Irish water spaniel and the friend of my childhood. I spent hours crying and tickling his tummy as he sprawled on his back on the sitting-room floor. Later that day he was taken to the vet's for the last time.

Luckily, nobody told me, 'He was only a dog.' Only a dog . . . only a being, who offered unconditional love, silent listening and complete acceptance. Nobody said that even more hurtful remark – 'Get another one.' As if dogs were like cars. As if you could just go out and buy a newer model.

As the *Daily Telegraph*'s pet agony aunt I often receive letters from people who are locked into an almost suicidal grief and anger at the loss of an animal friend. It has usually been made worse by somebody telling them they should not be grieving. Occasionally, they have told themselves that their grief is excessive. Yet it must be natural to grieve at the loss of a good friend. Sometimes I think the relationship between a human and an animal is closer than the friendship between human and human. It is a love without words and therefore without lies.

The loss of an animal friend is a real bereavement, whatever unthinking people may say. I send a sympathy card if somebody writes to me about the death of a pet, as a mark of respect for their pain. When we have lost an animal, our grief should be understood and permitted, rather than mocked or discounted.

This book pays tribute to the relationship between animals and their humans. It gives those who read it permission to grieve in their turn. The stories are a memorial to the happiness that we have enjoyed with our animals.

Celia Haddon, May 2006

Introduction

The night my companion of some 16 years died, I paced the floor in an agony of grief. How could I go on? I didn't think many people would understand the pain caused by the loss of a few pounds of black and white fur – even if they had met Brains the MagnifiCat, a little animal with great cattitude. How foolish I was. As friends and near strangers shared happy, moving and funny memories of their special animals, it dawned on me that a collection of these tales would be a tribute to Brains, and the other animals, and might help people as they mourned the loss of their own pet.

The book grew, taking in stories from people who work professionally with animals at London Zoo, Battersea Dogs and Cats Home, and the Blue Cross, and people with a public profile, such as Jilly Cooper, Ann Widdecombe and David Blunkett, who care passionately about animal welfare. So, while recognising that owning a pet will undoubtedly end in tears, *Farewell, my Lovely* celebrates also the boundless fun, pure joy and unquestioning love which an animal brings into your life – at whatever age, but perhaps more so when you are ill or getting on in years, which is why a percentage of any proceeds from the sale of this book will go to The Cinnamon Trust, an organisation which helps the elderly and infirm nationwide care for their pets.

Perhaps *Farewell, my Lovely* might also encourage others to take on a pet, not lightly, because a pet is for life as well as love, a feeling better summarised in the words of a young workman I met years ago, a few seconds after I'd encountered his delightful spaniel. 'She cost me a fortune,' he said, returning her adoring gaze, 'but to me, she is priceless.'

Susie Cornfield

If you have men who will exclude any of God's creatures from the shelter of compassion and pity, you will have men who deal likewise with their fellow men.

Not to hurt our humble brethren is our first duty to them, but to stop there is not enough. We have a higher mission – to be of service to them wherever they require it.

St Francis of Assisi

Hercules, the mouse and Brimble, the dog

Averil Jarvis, MBE, founder and director, The Cinnamon Trust

I have eight dogs and love them all for different reasons. They've taught me more about life and love than any human could. One of my dogs brought me this tiny baby wood mouse which I thought was dead and put in the dustbin. Later, I went to throw something away and saw the mouse open its mouth. I couldn't believe it. I took it out; it was blind in one eye and one front leg was dislocated badly. Using tweezers, I fed it oat flakes soaked in milk and, remarkably, it survived the night. There was only one name for this mouse – Hercules. The vet said nothing could be done for something so itsy bitsy so I brought Hercules home and someone I met on a walk made him a large oak house, with its own front door, dining room and bedroom.

The house had earth, straw and flowers on the floors and I used bottle tops for dishes. There were little wooden logs and loo roll tunnels to play in and only one tiny corner was ever soiled. Three weeks later, Hercules stood up, his bad leg mended. It was the best present on earth. Four days later, he looked at me with both eyes. I knew I'd witnessed a miracle.

I don't think Hercules would've survived in the wild, never having been taught what to do, but I never sought to tame him and he never showed any inclination to escape. He grew very fussy: not for him ordinary peas, they had to be *petit pois*. And if the choice of fare was not suitable, he threw his milk and water all over the place. I gave him seasonal berries, things I'd find in the garden or in the wild. He flourished and I adored him. I had him five years. Then one day I brought him an acorn I'd found in a hedgerow, which made him sick, and he died. The vet said it was paraquat, a highly poisonous weedkiller, and there was no antidote. To me, it was an absolute tragedy and you don't get over it, you just learn to come to terms with it. I went back to the hedgerow, which the poison spray had now turned brown, and thought what an indictment it was of what humans do.

But what's new? I was acquainted with an elderly lady who had an old Pyrenean mountain dog and a very nervous collie, both of whom she adored and took for walks three or four times a day. When she died, her body wasn't discovered for three days and the people who broke in found two terrified dogs who were immediately branded vicious and locked up in cold, dreadful kennels before being put down in not the kindest of ways. I was haunted by this event. I believed it to be utterly wrong, an absolute iniquity, that people should be forced to spend the end of their life without a beloved pet, and equally, that an old pet which had lost its owner should be put down or rehoused thoughtlessly.

The more I researched, the more I realised that people, even in their seventies, were anxious about having a pet, for fear of what might happen if they fell ill, became housebound, had to go into a home, or died. The solution was so simple but I didn't want to do it. I was happy, I was running a posh kennels, everything was going well for me, but, after 12 months of intense soul-searching and serious research, I sold up and established The Cinnamon Trust in 1985, named after my very special and much-beloved corgi.

I started with a small base, an Olivetti typewriter, a cardboard box and me. It was a hand-to-mouth existence and I had ghastly nightmares about how I was going to survive. But I'm stubborn, so today we have two sanctuaries, a new HQ building, 33 paid staff, and more than 7,500 volunteers nationwide, working individually or on a rota, looking after the pets of elderly or infirm people, sparing whatever time they can to walk a dog, feed a budgie, take a cat to the vet, or foster a pet when the owner is in hospital.

In this way, over the years, The Cinnamon Trust has helped elderly and terminally ill owners care for hundreds of thousands of animals, mostly cats and dogs and birds, but also a small pack of alpacas, and a homestead of 80-plus rabbits, each one known by name by their owner. We help animals continue to have a healthy, happy life, and we connect two people, an owner and a volunteer, as they sit over a cup of tea and talk about the pet they both care about. Sometimes, we ask an older bereaved owner to foster a pet who has lost its owner, which can help them both through a difficult time. And although we act only with the owner's consent (unless they're unconscious in hospital), we get referrals from doctors, social services, Macmillan nurses and the police. We're self-funded through donations, legacies and supporters' fundraising.

My faith, as well as many experiences I've had over the years, tell me that our animals are with us in an afterlife.

A strange thing happened not long after I started The Cinnamon Trust. The first dog to properly trial the first sanctuary was Brimble, a 14-year-old cocker spaniel, whose owner died. She'd obviously been much loved by him and she was a happy, gorgeous dog who readily woo-wooed with pleasure. At 18 she got pneumonia and although she recovered and was happy, she was frail and she'd stopped woo-wooing and pottered about, instead of going for long walks.

One day, I was taking a tray of dinners out to the dogs when Brimble started woo-wooing, which she hadn't done for weeks. I thought her tail would drop off, it was wagging so much. Her eyes and ears were alert, she was jumping up and down, and running alongside the fence. I felt a shiver go down my spine. She was greeting somebody I couldn't see. I knew I was going to lose her and she died the next day. But equally, I know from the pure delight emanating from that dog that she was greeting her dad who'd come to fetch her.

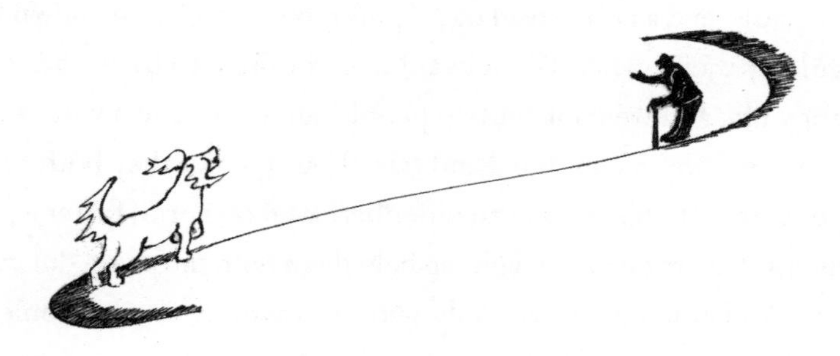

The Trap

E. G. C. Beckwith (from The Quill*, a British Prisoner-of-War magazine)*

"Snap!"
Goes the trap
Under my bed.
One feeble kick
(Which makes me rather sick)
And yet another mouse –
A tiny neighbour of my prison house –
Is dead,
And by my hand.
I'm sorry:
I did not understand,
It never struck me, when I went to get it
(That beastly trap), and baited it, and set it,
That you and I were somewhat on a par;
Nay, more, you were superior by far
In one respect, you funny little beast,
For you at least
Were free.
And who were we
To grudge such trifles as your fancy lit on?
Sampling your rations betwixt either mandible
You'd thought them dull, and stale (quite understandable
If hardly patriotic), and you hit on
This venture, to provide
A change for your diminutive inside.

Thoughtless, I only saw
You'd had a gnaw
At my provisions – chocolate, and cheese;
(My fault, of course for these
I should have put, for safety, in
A tin.)
I should indeed have thought of this before.
You are no more,
And no regrets can mend again, alack!
Your broken back.
How to atone for this untimely crime?
I'll think before I act another time;
And, when I take your carcase to its pyre
(The kitchen fire),
Old chap,
I'll add the trap.

Requiem for Pluto

Anon

One large-sized collar hanging by the door
And one lead seldom used, now not needed any more.
One food bowl with Dog on it that you were using yesterday,
A lonely walk without you – but you were with me every moment of the way,
One newly-filled-in grave near the clothesline and the red May tree,
One heart very badly broken – and that belongs to me.

Mabel, the cat

David Crombie, gardener

We had a telephone call from a friend telling us of a cat which for the past six months had been living rough under a hedge. It seemed okay but with winter approaching and as our previous cat had passed on, they wondered . . .

We said yes, and they captured the cat and put her in their stables where she found a carpet tube to hide in. Although her rear end stuck out, she seemed quite comfortable so it was decided we'd leave her there for the time being. Our friends fed her, she got bigger and couldn't get into the tube any more so, in the October, we brought her home. We called her Mabel after the character in the Broadway musical, *Mack and Mabel*.

Mabel lived behind the settee for about four weeks, with her food and litter tray; she would not be tempted out. Then, for some reason, she moved upstairs into the wardrobe in our bedroom. So we put her box and food in there, and left the wardrobe door open. She'd had to have a lot of dental work and had only two incisors left. We'd wake up in the night to hear this prolonged, very noisy sucking coming from inside the wardrobe as she tried to eat. Eventually, she ventured into the kitchen for her food and to use the litter tray but, immediately after, she'd shoot back upstairs. It was very rare that she went outside of the house.

Mabel soon learnt to trust my wife, Sue, but it took a long time for her to learn to trust me. She'd cringe, as though she was waiting to be walloped. We felt so sorry for her; she must have been to hell and back. She was silent yet full of character. Everybody asked after her and some saw her watching them from a window and disappear the moment she saw them look back at her. She never made a sound, never miaowed, never made any demands whatsoever, but she was always purring. She must have felt content and safe. Perhaps she felt she'd found a sanctuary.

We'd had Mabel for two years and three months when she started putting on a lot of weight. Our vet diagnosed a cancerous tumour and said that she was old and probably had had enough. It made my blood run cold to hear that. I thought she'd been let down so many times, I felt desperate to explain to her what was going on and why. But I knew she had to be put to sleep then and there, because I wouldn't have the courage to go back.

The next few days were just appalling. For 48 hours, Sue and I made a conscious decision to talk as though she were there. We had her cremated and her ashes are inside a little box in a family field where our other cats are. Sue didn't want the ashes scattered because she knew Mabel would feel safer if she were contained. In the same way, we still leave the wardrobe door open because somehow it feels right.

People say she was lucky to find us. I think the reverse is true. Mabel was a very fine cat.

Lonely House

Anon

No more cat tracks on the floor,
Muddy scratches on the door,
Puffs of hair upon the stairs,
Lacy fretwork on the chairs,

Indentations on my bed,
Markings where she laid her head,
Smudges on the window-pane
Showing where she watched in vain.

Haunts where she was wont to lay
Remind us that she is away.
My house is neater, that is true,
But, oh, how still and empty, too!

Daisy, the rabbit

Charlotte Middleditch, schoolgirl

I was seven and Victoria, my sister, was 10 when my mum took us to a pet shop in town. My sister saw a rabbit she wanted but I wanted it, too. I think I got her to change her mind by making a massive fuss. I wanted that particular rabbit because, as we stood by her cage, she jumped over to me, and this sounds stupid, but I felt we had a connection. So, Victoria got Dandelion and I got Daisy, a beautiful Dutch rabbit, half golden ginger, half white.

At first, I was really scared to pick her up because I didn't want to hurt her so when we got home I got Victoria to show me what to do. Then I went to check on Daisy every half-hour, and played with her and cuddled her.

The two rabbits didn't get on and they'd pull out each other's fur. Dandelion was sweet and gentle but Daisy was adventurous and had attitude. I liked her for that. When she was let out into the garden, she'd try to dig tunnels into our neighbour's garden and she tried to dig tunnels under her hutch. When we got close enough to catch her she'd stomp her two back feet to tell us to go away.

Dandelions were her favourite food and she liked carrots, grass, lettuce and cucumber. She'd eat anything, but not the packet food, the stuff that looks like muesli. She hated that.

I was really keen to teach her tricks – like jumping up the stairs, so that she could get into my room. I'm sure she knew it was my room and not anyone else's. But I got told off for that. She was allowed downstairs, but only in winter when it was cold.

I loved the way Skipper, my mum's godmother, and Daisy got on so well. Because of Skipper's health, she wasn't allowed to have an animal and Daisy would sit peacefully on her lap, without budging, for ages. I think that was nice for Skipper.

I had Daisy for five years and looked after her, fed her and cleaned out her cage until I had more to do at school. The day she died, Mum didn't tell me until she picked me up from school. Apparently, Mum'd gone out to feed Daisy and seen the top of the cage had been chewed away and all that was left of Daisy was her head. She'd been eaten by a fox. I ran out into the garden, crying. We all cried.

When Dandelion had died, we'd had a service and a grave, and played the song from *Titanic,* but for Daisy we didn't have a body, so Victoria, Mummy, Daddy and me stood in the garden and we remembered things about Daisy, like the time we brought her in for Christmas and she peed under the tree because she must've thought it was real. And the time we bought her a lead so we could take her for walks but it didn't fit because she was too fat.

It's three years since Daisy died and I still miss her. She was peaceful, patient and so cute. I used to come home from school and sit watching TV with her on my lap, cuddling her. I'd talk to her and she'd twitch her nose as though she heard what I was saying. I've got good friends and we talk about most things but I could talk to Daisy, tell her everything, and know she didn't tell anyone. I've got a photograph on my bookcase of us together, and I still think of her and still talk to her in my head.

Epitaph on a Hare

William Cowper
1731–1800

Here lies, whom hound did ne'er pursue,
Nor swifter greyhound follow,
Whose foot ne'er tainted morning dew,
Nor ear heard huntsman's hallo',

Old Tiney, surliest of his kind,
Who, nurs'd with tender care,
And to domestic bounds confin'd,
Was still a wild Jack-hare.

Though duly from my hand he took
His pittance ev'ry night,
He did it with a jealous look,
And, when he could, would bite.

His diet was of wheaten bread,
And milk, and oats, and straw,
Thistles, or lettuces instead,
With sand to scour his maw.

On twigs of hawthorn he regal'd,
On pippins' russet peel;
And, when his juicy salads fail'd,
Slic'd carrot please'd him well.

A Turkey carpet was his lawn,
Whereon he lov'd to bound,
To skip and gambol like a fawn,
And swing his rump around.

His frisking was at evening hours,
For then he lost his fear;
But most before approaching show'rs,
Or when a storm drew near.

Eight years and five round-rolling moons
He thus saw steal away,
Dozing out all his idle noons,
And ev'ry night at play.

I kept him for his humour' sake,
For he would oft beguile
My heart of thoughts that made it ache,
And force me to a smile.

But now, beneath this walnut-shade
He finds his long, last home,
And waits in snug concealment laid,
'Till gentler Puss shall come.

He, still more aged, feels the shocks
From which no care can save,
And, partner once of Tiney's box,
Must soon partake his grave.

Jack, the bird and Barley, the dog

Mark Habben, team leader, Animal Activities Department, London Zoo

Animals have been a life-long passion. When I was three or four I was turning over stones for worms, and looking for caterpillars, spiders and frogs. My father and both grandfathers were very encouraging. I think my mother's attitude is best described as extremely tolerant, especially when I was 11 and breeding snakes and the cat dislodged the lid from a glass cabinet, freeing 22 baby North American garter snakes into the house which we were still finding weeks later.

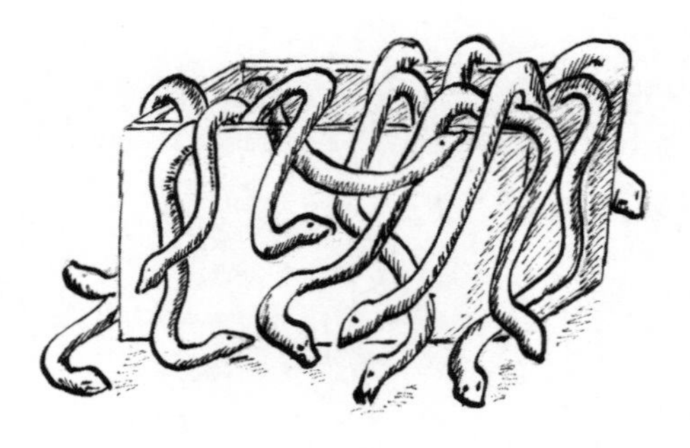

After a school-trip to London Zoo, I kept nagging my parents to take me back again and again, and once I said how much I wanted to live in the Keeper's Lodge, little knowing that a few years on, I'd be doing just that. I love London Zoo, not only for its history, being the first zoo in the world, but for its conservation and educational work. I got a job at the Zoo after doing a degree in animal biology and then took a six-month break to lead a group of volunteers researching wildlife in the Amazon, returning to the Zoo in this managerial position, working out programmes which encourage specific, natural behaviours in animals such as kangaroos and owls, meerkats and eagles, while providing the public with a view of their life.

We're encouraged not to get too attached to an animal but, that said, it's difficult not to form an attachment to some. I worked for six years with a kookaburra called Jack. I went into his cage every day to feed him, to exercise and fly him, or simply to see him. He was a beautiful bird, personable, feisty but gentle, and fun. He was also a natural performer. We'd throw food into the air above the heads of an audience of 700 and he'd fly up and catch it before it landed, often taking in a few insects along the way. He never missed. He had a phobia about helicopters, which in London is a bit of a problem. He'd fly off and huddle somewhere until the helicopter's noise was far away and he'd come down only when we shook his rubber snake. He'd swoop

down, grab hold of it and give it a thorough shaking, just as kookaburras do with real snakes in the wild, but really for longer than was absolutely necessary.

One day I was in early and thought it odd that I hadn't heard Jack's usual call, to which I'd always respond, so I went to check him out. He was sitting on the floor, surrounded in blood and feathers, and I realised one of his wings was damaged. I rushed to get the vet who examined him and said he'd never fly again and that the kindest thing was to euthanase him. I lifted him up, took him into the operating theatre and held him until he stopped breathing. It was heartbreaking and I can't say that I didn't shed a tear.

Kookaburras are very territorial and we found out later that Jack's injury had been caused by a fox which he'd seen off before, but not this time. For weeks afterwards, the staff were very subdued: the cage was empty and Jack left a void. But I like to remember him as he was – a happy bird.

At home, perhaps the best animals to get close to are dogs. They are absolutely fantastic; they'd do anything for you, no matter who or what you are. I had my first dog when I was 13 or 14 and I was so ecstatic when she arrived that I didn't want to go to school.

Barley was a stunningly beautiful cross Border collie and Labrador, like a little white fox when she was a pup. She was a real head turner and I called every friend I could think of to come and take a look at her. She was intelligent and obedient; she never needed to be on a lead. And she was always there with a comforting paw, seeming to know your mood or if you'd had a bad day.

She was also a lady. I used to take her on walks and on bird-watching trips where she'd sit quietly beside me, as she did with my dad when he took her to the pub. The only thing she hated was water. If we were out on a walk and it started to rain, that was one thing, but if we tried to set off when it was raining, she'd sit on the doorstep and wouldn't budge. She hated getting her paws wet. She avoided puddles. It was almost as if she expected us to lay down our coats on them for her. Bless her.

Barley was my constant companion for more than a decade and then last year, the night after Guy Fawkes, she did something she never did: she jumped on to the sofa and when my dad ordered her off, she jumped back up again. The next day my mum found her dead in the kitchen. We never did find out the specific cause of Barley's death but I think it's safe to say that it was a result of the noise of the fireworks, which she hated.

I felt physically sick when my mum told me the news, an emotional wreck. Barley was irreplaceable. The next day I went out on one of the walks we used to do together and carved Barley's name and date of birth on an oak tree we used to pass. I still do the walk. I like to check her name's still there. We lost her too young and I wanted to immortalise her.

Is there an after-life? Who's to say? If there is, it has to be inclusive of animals.

The Dead Sparrow

William Cartwright
1611–1643

Tell me not of joy; there's none,
Now my little Sparrow's gone:
He, just as you,
Would try and woo,
He would chirp and flatter me;
He would hang the wing awhile –
Till at length he saw me smile
Lord, how sullen he would be!

He would catch a crumb, and then
Sporting, let it go agen;
He from my lip
Would moisture sip;
He would from my trencher feed;
Then would hop, and then would run,
And cry *Philip* when he'd done.
O! whose heart can choose but bleed?

O how eager would he fight,
And ne'er hurt, though he did bite.
        No morn did pass,
        But on my glass
He would sit, and mark and do
What I did – now ruffle all
His feathers o'er, now let 'em fall;
And then straightaway sleek them too.

Whence will Cupid get his darts
Feathered now to pierce our hearts?
        A wound he may
        Not, Love, convey,
Now this faithful bird is gone;
O let mournful turtles join
With loving red-breasts, and combine
To sing dirges o'er his stone!

Dog's Death

John Updike
born 1932

She must have been kicked unseen or brushed by a car.
Too young to know much, she was beginning to learn
To use the newspapers spread on the kitchen floor
And to win, wetting there, the words, "Good dog! Good dog!"

We thought her shy malaise was a shot reaction.
The autopsy disclosed a rupture in her liver.
As we teased her with play, blood was filling her skin
And her heart was learning to lie down forever.

Monday morning, as the children were noisily fed
And sent to school, she crawled beneath the youngest's bed.
We found her twisted and limp but still alive.
In the car to the vet's, on my lap, she tried

To bite my hand and died. I stroked her warm fur
And my wife called in a voice imperious with tears.
Though surrounded by love that would have upheld her,
Nevertheless she sank and, stiffening, disappeared.

Back home, we found that in the night her frame,
Drawing near to dissolution, had endured the shame
Of diarrhoea and had dragged across the floor
To a newspaper carelessly left there. *Good dog.*

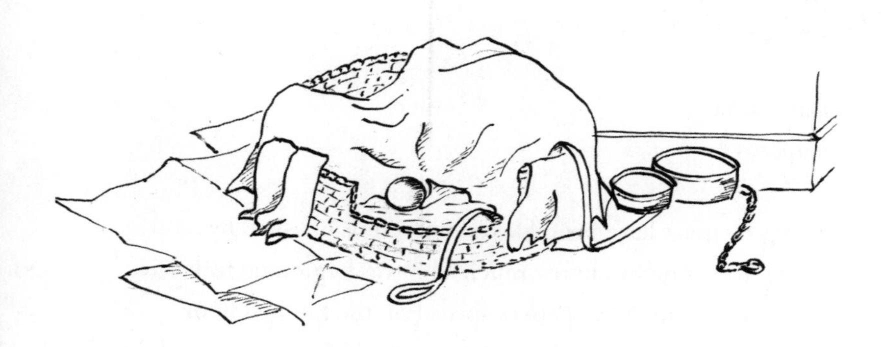

Fortnum, Hero et al, the dogs

Jilly Cooper, writer, broadcaster and media star

I remember Jamie, our Scottie dog, who had to be put down when I was four years old and my mother crying as if her heart were breaking. She'd lost relations and friends but she cried more over that little dog. Her face was carved up by grief and I remember feeling embarrassed as well as wondering how to comfort her. There was Penny, a Sealyham, Freckles, a springer spaniel, and Simmie, a golden retriever, who was a terrible wanderer. We got a call one day from the local cinema to say that he'd been shaking hands with the projectionist for the last half-hour and could we come and get him so that they could start the film.

Later, there was Fortnum, a mongrel, who had sex with every bitch he encountered and fought every dog he met. I loved him passionately but I had to have him put down after he killed a dog. It was dreadful, absolutely dreadful. In his early life, he'd had to be cut down from a cross; a gang of louts had tried to crucify him. The next owner who took him in found that he cried whenever she left him. She was on her way to take him to Battersea Dogs and Cats Home when I met her. I took him in then and there. We had him about six years.

Barbara was an offspring of one of his sprees. I remember she had a very vulgar curly tail which, after we moved to the country, was stung by a wasp and fell into a long, curved patrician lurcher's tail. There was also Mabel, Bessie and Hero, who was my heroine. She was beautiful, elegant and charming, although she bit Leo most mornings (well, he does have heavy feet), and actually bit quite a lot of other people. But it was fear-biting, because she was very, very shy and came to me as a puppy when she'd just lie in my arms, utterly helpless.

Perhaps because I couldn't have children, although we have two wonderful adopted children, my dogs have all been particularly special. And now they've gone, there are pictures of them everywhere in the house. In fact, I can't see myself in the bathroom mirror any more because of the pictures.

All of them, except Fortnum, who died in Putney, are in a graveyard by the tennis court. And they've all got their own epitaphs. Every time one of our animals dies, I sit down almost immediately and chronicle its life, habits and endearing tricks and its last hours, so I have about ten pages on each. I recommend it as a way of preserving memories, which might otherwise be lost.

Hero died at the end of last year and this is the first time in 35 years that I've been without a dog. It's ghastly. The only flipside is that, thriving on new attention, our five cats have blossomed. With five of them, I have to have a stroking rota in case they get jealous. There is more room on the bed and Leo doesn't get bitten when he reaches out for me in the middle of the night, but it feels so empty when you go for a walk without a dog.

There's so much anti-dog attitude about nowadays, fines here and there in parks and outside people's homes, but I think you

get colossal amounts of uncritical love from a dog, as well as fun, merriment, cuddles and endless companionship. And I've made friends with people I've met walking the dogs, friends now of 30 years' standing.

My dogs have seen me through so many difficult times and they've also helped me really learn about and appreciate wildlife, trees and flowers I observe on my walks. While I was taking them out late at night, I also taught myself the stars.

A kind friend wants to give me a lurcher pup for Christmas, but I'm trying to be strong and wait till the summer. I've got a huge book coming out and with all the publicity running up to publication and a three-week book tour after that, it wouldn't be fair on a new dog to keep leaving it when it'd only just arrived. I am actually hoping to get two dogs so they can be companions, and when one dies you don't have an utterly dog-less house, as I have now.

I like the idea that when you die and, hopefully, reach heaven, all your animals come bounding over a sunlit lawn to greet you. Do I believe they're there in an after-life? Yes, yes, of course. You have to believe that, don't you? It's just too awful to think one won't see one's dogs again.

Jilly Cooper's book Animals in War *was written to accompany the first Animals in War exhibition at the Imperial War Museum in 1983, and all royalties from it go to the Animals in War Memorial Fund. The memorial is in Park Lane, London.*

An Epitaph

Lord Byron
1788–1824

Near this spot
Are deposited the remains of one
Who possessed beauty without vanity,
Strength without insolence,
Courage without ferocity,
And all the virtues of man without his vices.

This praise, which would be unmeaning flattery
If inscribed over human ashes,
Is but a just tribute to the memory of
Boatswain, a dog.

Inscription on a monument
at Newstead Abbey

Rover, the fish

Jonathan Stone, accountant

Aside from my brother, I lived an animal-free life until my mid-thirties when I decided I wanted some fish. I did the research and got a tank, 4ft by 2ft 6in., a pump, some rocks and underwater toys and then a goldfish I called Fido and a blue koi carp, about the length of a pencil, which I called Rover.

Rover and Fido were a pleasure to have around. They were beautiful to look at and were very low maintenance. They were peaceful; they didn't answer back. They didn't complain about my music, didn't mind if I came home late and, unlike me, weren't faddish about their food.

I lost Fido after 18 months and I buried him in the garden. For years it was just me and Rover. Then I got burgled. Sometimes I wonder if the shock of it all killed Rover. He went off his food, started swimming backwards and began to look poorly. So one day I put him into a large, 550 gram jar, punched holes in the lid, and very slowly drove him to the vet.

The surgery was full of cats and dogs and rabbits and I think a fish was the last thing the vet was expecting. He opened the jar and began pouring out the water but, instead of landing in a tiny metal container, Rover slithered all round the table before either of us could get hold of him. Then the vet put a two-inch syringe into his flesh, behind his gill, and I took him home and put him back in his tank. I kept an eye on him as I had my supper. He did not look in the best of health. The next morning I found him floating on top of the water.

I put him in a box and buried him, near Fido, at the bottom of the garden. I was upset. We'd been together, man and fish, for a good few years. I'd have liked to have given him a Viking funeral, put him in a small boat at sunset and pushed him out to sea, but that kind of thing isn't possible in south London.

I had a few other fish – Metro, Maestro and Mini – but not one matched up to Rover.

If God Had Wanted a Gerbil

Anon

If God had wanted a gerbil
He should have saved up like me
And gone to the pet shop and bought one
That's doing things properly.

If God had wanted a gerbil
Then I think it awfully mean
To have made me drop mine and kill it
When I fed it and kept it so clean.

If God had wanted a gerbil
He should have taken its cage and straw
No, I won't have another gerbil
Just in case God wants some more.

Tommy, the tortoise and Jeremy, the tortoise

Diana Eccleston, writer, and a former controller for the RSPCA

I grew up in the 1950s with a very sweet, all-black Labrador cross, a rescue dog from Battersea Dogs and Cats Home. I was five when the vet came to the house to put him down and that was the first time I saw my father cry. I felt sad, twice over. I was given a puppy – a dachshund, aptly named Crackers – who became fixated on my mother and would hurl himself at the door when she went out and scratch it to bits. One day, I came home from school and was told that Crackers had been given away and I was given a hamster, which I found very dull and no substitute.

Every year, we'd get a new tortoise. My mother would go to Brixton Market to buy potatoes and carrots, etc., and then, at another stall, she'd buy a tortoise for 15p in today's money. They were the focus of attention when friends came to play but the poor things were lucky to see out the year because, in those days, they were imported in sack-loads, in terrible conditions, and no one had any idea what to feed them or how to care for them.

Losing Tommy, the tortoise, was my first real and lasting experience of death. I remember sitting on the concrete by the back door, holding him and hoping the warmth of the sun would bring him back to life. My mother had to prise him away from me.

I told my brother to chip in with his pocket money to buy a companion for our new tortoise because, whatever the experts say, I was and remain convinced tortoises are happier with company. A lone tortoise is prone to wander off when it gets the urge to seek a mate. For me, the proof is the three healthy tortoises I've had for more than 40 years.

I think tortoises make a garden feel more lived in as they chunter about, ploughing down the flowers, and crashing shells when it's hot and they feel randy. And I love their prehistoric appeal: old as the hills yet unthreatening in the way reptiles such as snakes and crocodiles are. They aren't exactly cuddly but they can be very friendly, charging up to you like puppies when they get to know your sound and think you have food for them.

Not that long ago, I lost Jeremy, one of my golden oldies, who died in hibernation and I'm not sure why or how. I was devastated because I loved him so much. He was small and friendly, a nice compact shape, and was always quick to put his head out of his shell for a tickle. And I was proud of him being the dad of the eggs which his partner, Titania, laid. She's a strong character, polite and ladylike. She'll wait until everyone else has had their fill before she eats. She's regal is Titania. She and Jeremy made a lovely pair.

Baby Tortoise

(an extract)

D. H. Lawrence
1885–1930

You know what it is to be born alone
Baby tortoise!
The first day to heave your feet little by little from the shell,
Not yet awake,
And remain lapsed on earth,
Not quite alive.

A tiny, fragile, half-animate bean.

To open your tiny beak-mouth, that looks as if it would never
open,

Like some iron door;
To lift the upper hawk-beak from the lower base
And reach your skinny little neck
And take your first bite at some dim bit of herbage,
Alone, small insect,
Tiny bright-eye,
Slow one.

The foster-mum

Mary Black, volunteer, Battersea Dogs and Cats Home

I visited Battersea Dogs and Cats Home about four years ago with a friend who was thinking of getting a dog. I hadn't realised they dealt also with cats and I wandered off to have a look. It was impressive. The cages were heated and had colourful blankets. The whole place looked cheerful and at the back of my mind, I thought that when I retired I'd like to be involved in some way. Then I saw a cat, as still as a statue, looking utterly miserable. I had to have her. I was interviewed about my home and situation, advised that this little cat might be ideal in the long run but, initially, could be big trouble. That didn't dissuade me. Neither did the fact that they had to take her out of her cage with long, industrial-strength gloves. For six months Rosie lived under a cabinet, coming out only to use a litter tray. Four years on, she's here in the room, sitting between us on a blanket, while we talk. And Rocco, my other Battersea cat, adores her.

Three near-dead stray cats have landed on my doorstep over the years, and there have always been animals in my life. One set of grandparents had a farm, my parents always had a dog, and when my children were small and because I worked, we had cats because I thought it a good idea to teach the children that if they have an animal they must care for it and respect it until it dies.

So when I gave up work four years ago, I wrote to Battersea, offering to help out in whatever way they needed. After an interview, and a tetanus jab from my GP, I became a volunteer.

I go into Battersea one day a week, as a socialiser, which means brushing and cuddling cats and kittens, and talking to them, preparing them for a life in a new home.

Battersea has four 'cat' areas – reception, where new arrivals are checked out thoroughly by the vets and kept for about a week or more; mums and kittens; the isolation unit, where no volunteer who has pets at home is allowed; and the sales department.

It was about a year ago when I overheard the kennel staff talking about a particular cat and her six kittens. Fostering is an important element in Battersea's work: some long-stay animals go downhill suddenly; they get depressed living in cages. I must have mentioned that I had a spare room . . . within 24 hours, the family had moved into my house, with a large transporter cage and the food that Battersea provides to fosterers, and a list of emergency contact phone numbers.

What was it like? Well, the mother of my current litter taught her brood to use the litter tray at a very early stage, but with the first family there was pee everywhere so I learnt to cover the floor with newspaper and use a lining underneath! But

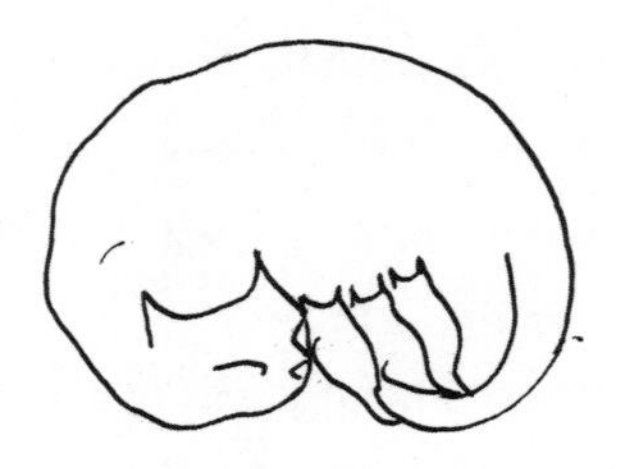

they're adorable; huge time wasters as you sit and play with them, and watch them develop. They certainly have more visitors than I normally get. And Rosie and Rocco don't mind, as long as their little lives are not interrupted.

Cats behave differently when they become mothers. As well as a new litter, which can be demanding, they're always hungry, always on the look-out for food. And at Battersea, as well as being a stray, lost, or brought in by owners who can no longer care for them, they're coping with different surroundings, which change again when they're fostered out. It can all be quite unsettling, so they need a lot of care and understanding.

After about six weeks, the mother of my first litter was ready to return to Battersea; the weaned kittens followed a few weeks later. That was a terrible, terrible time. I cried my eyes out. I'd got very fond of them, and I missed them a lot, even though I was glad not to do the work. After nine weeks, I did and do feel possessive about them all. No matter how ordinary some might be, I think they are all stars. And, yes, I never think any owner is going to be good enough! It is a form of bereavement. I cry a great deal every time I have to have one of my own cats put to sleep. But I tell myself that I've given them as good a life as I could and being put out of pain is something we humans can as yet not ask for.

One gets over it. And I remind myself of the reason why

I foster: to give a home to animals, especially ones with large litters; to give them peace and quiet, and room to thrive and play; a more natural environment that more easily acclimatises and socialises them.

Do I get tempted to keep one? Yes! But in my house, I couldn't have three cats and foster. So, I tell myself I can't have them but that I am giving them the best start in life that I possibly can.

Little Paws

Anon

This is a prayer for little paws
All up and down the land:
Driven away, no friendly voice,
Never an outstretched hand.

For weary little paws of beasts
Torn and stained with red,
And never a home and never a rest
Till little beasts are dead.

O God of homeless things,
look down
And try to ease the way
Of all the little weary paws
That walk the world today.

Sparky, the rat

Kelham Salter, sports policy researcher

I was about nine when my mum took me to a pet shop. I wanted something a bit different, that no one else at school had, and that didn't intrude because my dad isn't that keen on animals. And there were these tiny newborn rats, the cheapest pets in the shop. My mum was a bit taken aback but they looked so sweet . . .

So Sparky came home and was with us for about four years. She lived in a cage in my bedroom and every day, when I came home from school, I let her out. She was unbelievably tame, with a defined personality. I'd say she had the character of a friendly dog. She loved attention. She'd sit on my shoulder or in the pocket of my jumper. And I know 100 per cent that she recognised me, and my mum. I cooked her whole chocolate cakes, the only thing I could cook. I might have had bits of the cake but I cooked it for her.

When I went off to boarding school, mum looked after her. Mum loved Sparky every bit as much as I did and fed her Weetabix and milk, or bread soaked in warm milk. Sparky might not have cost very much and she was certainly very low maintenance, but when she developed cancer, twice, it was out of the question that she'd be put to sleep. My mum would not let that happen. Sparky had proper operations, the works. The vet had never known anything like it.

Sparky died one Monday after I'd returned to school, and was buried in our garden. I had another rat but I didn't feel the same about her, she just wasn't Sparky. Sparky was part of our household, part of our family.

Stray Goat

Elizabeth Montagu
1720–1800
from a letter to the Duchess of Portland, 17th December, 1738

I heard a very ridiculous story a few days ago: Mr Page, brother to Sir Gregory, going to visit Mr Edward Walpole, a tame goat which was in the street followed him unperceived when he got out of the coach into the house. Mr Walpole's servant, thinking the goat came out of Mr Page's coach, carried it into the room to Mr Walpole, who thought it a little odd Mr Page should bring such a visitor, as Mr Page no less admired his choice of so savoury a companion; but civility, a great disguiser of sentiments, prevented their declaring their opinions, and the goat, no respecter of persons or furniture, began to rub himself against the frame of a chair which was carved and gilt, and the chair, which was fit for a Christian, but unable to bear the shock of a beast, fell almost to pieces. Mr Walpole thought Mr Page very indulgent to his dear crony the goat, and wondering he took no notice of the damage, said he fancied tame goats did a great deal of harm, to which the other said he believed so too: after much free and easy behaviour of the goat, to the great detriment of the furniture, they came to an explanation, and Mr Goat was turned downstairs . . .

Teddy, the dog

David Blunkett, MP for Sheffield Brightside

Meeting Teddy was an amazing experience. The sheer size of him compared to Ruby (a previous dog) warmed my heart. Here was a dog whose body was so far off the ground that I was bound to feel if he were trying to pick scraps off the pavement or his movements indicated that he had become distracted. Here was a dog – a chocolate-coloured, curly coat retriever/Labrador cross – who needed brushing, but did not shed golden hairs all over the carpet, furniture and my trousers. Here was a dog who appeared not to be obsessed with food and took a genuine interest in where I wanted to go. My sort of dog. He was big and magnificent, and also extremely fast. Immediately we began training together I started to lose weight . . .

I was constantly astonished by Teddy's willingness to work and his dedication to getting the job done: looking out for my needs rather than his own, plodding along when the going was easy and searching out the best ways when it was difficult . . . Teddy was a workaholic, which made us well matched . . .

Teddy had been with me for the best part of nine years and was already well known in the Palace of Westminster. Having learned by trial and error to find our way through the vast maze of corridors and staircases, we had soon mastered our regular routes sufficiently to allow us to go about our business with reasonable confidence and aplomb. With my election as an MP, Teddy was set to become the first dog allowed on the floor of the Common's Chamber proper.

There was, however, a dark cloud hanging over us: Teddy's declining health due to old age. Could he withstand the long hours and pressure of my first year in Parliament? Even at the age of eleven, his commitment and loyalty made him as eager as ever for work. Whenever the lead and harness were taken off their hook, he would be beside me, putting his head into his harness rather than waiting for me to pass it over his head. It was deeply touching. He was determined not to be left at home or to give up. He was less robust than in his youth and slightly stiffer in the joints, but otherwise not in bad shape.

After soul-searching discussions with the GDBA (Guide Dogs for the Blind Association), and since the vet assured me that Teddy was in no serious discomfort, it was agreed that he should continue working as long as he was keen to do so . . .

As the weeks turned into months, tiredness took its toll: I was struck down with viral pneumonia, which led to a spell in hospital . . . had it not been for the fact that I was forced to spend time in hospital recuperating, thereby providing an enforced rest for Teddy, I doubt whether he could have gone on working for me as long as he did, for by this time I had noticed he was beginning to slow down. I left hospital in March 1988 under doctor's orders to take things easy, and in the weeks that followed Teddy and I made our way round Westminster looking for all the world like a pair of geriatrics.

Then one hot, humid day in the middle of May, I noticed that Teddy was panting, not abnormally at first, but as the day faded and the air temperature dropped, he seemed to grow much worse. Desperately concerned, I carried him out of the Palace of Westminster and took him in a taxi to the nearest vet.

The prognosis could scarcely have been worse. Teddy's

heart and circulation were failing – he had only a few weeks to live. I literally dropped everything and with a heavy heart took Teddy by train back to Sheffield. There I left him with Valda and Trevor, who I knew would love and care for him . . . I reluctantly returned to London, where I tried my best to concentrate on the tasks in hand. It was not easy.

On 5 July, as the House of Commons was debating a motion on the fortieth anniversary of the National Health Service, I was given a message that Teddy had been rushed to the vet after collapsing and losing the use of his legs. The vet felt that he had at last come to the end of the road and that it would be kinder to put him to sleep. I had to return home at once. Without waiting for permission to be absent from the vote, I caught the next train north. When I arrived at the surgery, Teddy tried to get to his feet and I will never forget the sound of his paws scrabbling on the bare lino of the surgery floor. My heart went out to him. Despite some reluctance on the part of the vet, I managed to persuade him to allow us to take Teddy home to familiar surroundings. I did not want Teddy's days to end there in that surgery.

Once out of the car Teddy found the strength from somewhere to make his own way into the house and on to his favourite rug. When the vet arrived a couple of hours later, I cradled Teddy's head in my lap and gently fondled his ears as he was put to sleep. There is a lump in my throat as I write even after all this time. I have to admit that on that evening, with all the memories of Teddy flooding back, I became the sentimentalist I had so scorned in others twenty years earlier, before I had a dog . . .

In the days following Teddy's death, as the news spread, many kind friends and colleagues expressed their condolences, but none was more unexpected than a handwritten message from Margaret Thatcher saying how sorry she was that Teddy had died and that she understood what a great loss it would be for me, not only for practical reasons but also for the loss of the enormous affection guide dogs have for the owner . . .

Teddy had become equally widely known outside Parliament and so many sacks of letters arrived from sympathetic members of the public that a fund was set up in his memory. This raised over £7,600 for the GDBA and helped provide training for several new guide dogs, one of whom was to be named Teddy. I am sure 'the gentle giant' would have liked that since he had no sons of his own.

Extracts from David Blunkett's autobiography,
On A Clear Day,
used with his kind permission.

Jimmy, The Dog In My Life

(an extract)

Sir Arthur Bryant
1899–1985

Perhaps the most poignant of all memories of this beloved companion is that of the intense anxiety, and, when anxiety gave place to the knowledge that he was not to be left behind, joy with which he set out on journeys. Long before the hour of departure he would have mounted guard on the piled luggage in the hall, passionately resolute not to be left behind. Indeed, as he grew older it became quite impossible to leave home without him. And when train journeys – a far more comfortable mode of travelling with him as companion – succeeded car journeys, with what eagerness, despite old age and infirmity, did he stand in the taxi, swaying on his master's knees as it sped towards Waterloo, and with what tremendous barking, still remembered by the porters there, he entered that station, temporarily drowning every sound in the vast, echoing space but his own triumphant announcement of his coming. That so much noise could come from that minute, frail white form was something of a miracle.

I like to think that at the crack of doom I shall hear that sound again. That inseparable friend of so many years – or rather the casket containing his ashes – lies now beneath the turf of a West Country lawn looking down a valley where Dorset and Wiltshire meet and in whose woods he had often hunted rabbit, fox and badger. Gone are the sad last memories of vet and injection and the growing pain and infirmity of those last years – so bravely and patiently borne. There only remains the recollection of an unquenchable vitality and capacity for life, above all for love and loyalty, and of something which for want of a better word I can only call nobility. True to his nature as a dog – fierce, independent, proud and predatory – he displayed towards the humans who befriended him a trust, a selfless tenderness and devotion that nothing could alter and which as much as any experience of life, has convinced me that, in some mysterious way beyond our understanding, love is eternal.

Calypso Dancer, the horse

Mary Middleton, accountant

As a child growing up in south London suburbs, I always wanted a dog but my mother flatly refused and it wasn't until I was in the sixth form at school that I got to know a dog which belonged to my boyfriend's family. They lived on the edge of the countryside, and I realised that was the life I wanted – country, walks and a dog.

I've had about seven dogs but, that said, for nearly 30 years of my life I had a horse, the perfect pet for a working person. A dog is wonderful but it's like a pre-school child that never grows up – you always have to be there for it. But a horse can be liveried, and someone else does the mucking out, grooming and feeding.

I took up riding seriously at university, choosing a college well out of London, and rode most evenings and weekends in Windsor Great Park. After that, I went twice a week to an extremely unorthodox riding establishment where you jumped everything, galloped, or charged through rivers. One day, the owner put me on her sister's pony, and from then on I never wanted to ride another horse and, for 30 years, rarely did.

I felt so safe and secure on her and, despite the fact that I fell off her time after time and that she was a cranky, irritable and wilful beast, she gave me confidence. Riding her was like getting into your favourite armchair.

She was 10 years old, 14.3 hands, a grey Connemara, and was called Calypso Dancer, among other things. The day they told me she was for sale, I went to the bank, and bought her that evening before they changed their minds.

She could turn on a sixpence, but only left-handed, and had two speeds: fast and stop. I remember one day, riding her in an open boggy ploughed field, when I waved through three racehorses. She chased after them like a thing possessed. I couldn't hold her back, and she kept going hell for leather over this terrible terrain until they'd disappeared from sight, at which point she pulled up, drenched in sweat.

She was getting older, losing her footing and getting panic attacks, when there was an incident when she was seriously spooked by a puddle and tipped me off so I was under her feet. I was injured, but it could've been much worse. I'd never been nervous of her in our 20-year relationship, but I was then.

I found an ideal retirement home for her and I rode her only in spring and autumn when the weather was temperate, and she was settled and happy. Then one winter she developed a sore on her backside which grew bigger and wouldn't heal, and the vet said, with spring approaching, and flies, it was better to let her go. The light had gone out of her eyes, she couldn't lift her head or her tail, and I couldn't bear it. I'd always been there for the dogs but . . .

The traditional method is to shoot horses; an injection can cause them to panic when their legs give way. Either way, I decided I couldn't cope. I went to work and left it to the vet, and to Calypso's stable girl. They told me she sank gently to the ground. I try not to think about it, but I hope that's how it really happened. I always gave her the best – cost and conventional wisdom didn't come into it.

Not long ago, I was out for a walk when I realised I knew exactly what it would feel like to be riding her across this unknown field with a curving track. It doesn't matter to me that I'll never ride again, I'll never lose that feeling; I'll never lose her. She is always there, in my consciousness.

Prayer of a Horse

Maurice Portal

"To you, my master, I offer my prayer. Feed me, water and care for me, and when the day's work is done provide me with shelter, and a clean dry bed, and a stall wide enough to lie down in comfort.

"Talk to me, and your voice often means as much to me as the reins.

"Pat me sometimes, that I may serve you more gladly and learn to love you. Do not whip me when going up hill, never strike or kick me, but give me a chance to understand your orders.

"Watch me, and if I fail to do your bidding, see if something is wrong with my harness or feet.

"Do not tie my head in an unnatural position or take away my best defence against the flies and mosquitoes by cutting off my tail, or limit my range of vision by blinding so that I am frightened by what I cannot see. And finally, O my master, when my youthful strength is gone, do not turn me out to starve or freeze, or sell me to some cruel master to be slowly tortured or starved to death.

"But do you my master take my life in the kindest way and your God will reward you here and hereafter; you will not consider me irreverent if I ask you in the name of Him who was born in a stable."

Gurami, the fish

James Stacey-Clear, estate agent

I'm about to lose one of a pair of guramis I bought when I set up my first tropical fish tank in my room at Northampton University four years ago. Her partner was a big orange-coloured bully who became better behaved when I introduced more fish. She used to change colour and markings from dark blue to white, dependent on her mood, but now she is old, and her fins and scales are showing signs of ageing.

My father is a keen fisherman and we always had a pond, and whenever we went to a fair, I came home with a goldfish. But I wasn't interested in catching fish, rather with life under the water, and how you can create a fish's environment in your own room. I've learnt a lot but if a fish is poorly I ask the aquarium shop for a diagnosis and water analysis.

Keeping tropical fish turned out to be a good chat-up line. And I found girlfriends really enjoyed coming along with me to garden centres to choose a new fish. But that wasn't why I kept them. They're easy to look after and, unlike dogs, which I love, they're not going to get up to much mischief, like rooting around

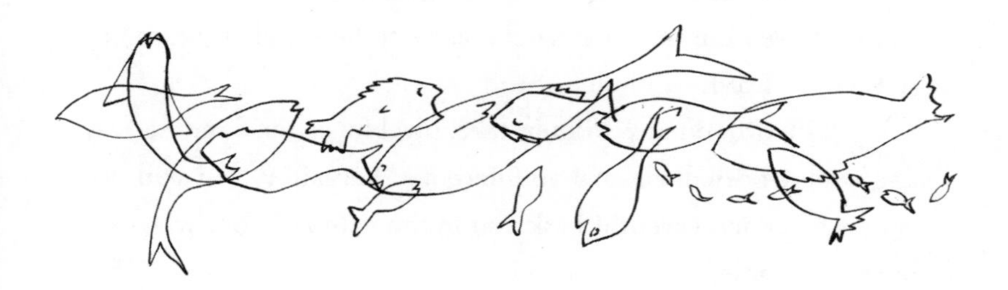

in bins or whatever. And they're very relaxing. I liked to watch the gurami and the others while I was studying and doing my dissertation.

Now I'm at work, the gurami lives with my 13 other fish in a large tank in my mother's hallway. Like the others, I feed her by hand. She's become less nervous, less shy, and rather clever in the way she avoids the other fish, checks out everything, and is at the front of the queue for food. I'll be sad when she dies but there's a special spot in Mum's garden where I'll bury her.

Rupert Brooke
1887–1915

Fish (fly-replete, in depth of June
Dawdling away their wat'ry noon)
Ponder deep wisdom, dark or clear,
Each secret fishy hope or fear.
Fish say, they have their Stream and Pond;
But is there anything Beyond?
This life cannot be All, they swear,
For how unpleasant, if it were!
One may not doubt that, somehow, good
Shall come of Water and of Mud;
And, sure, the reverent eye must see
A Purpose in Liquidity.

We darkly know, by Faith we cry,
The future is not Wholly Dry.
Mud unto Mud! – Death eddies near –
Not here the appointed End, not here!
But somewhere, beyond Space and Time,
Is wetter water, slimier slime!
And there (they trust) there swimmeth One
Who swam ere rivers were begun,
Immense, of fishy form and mind,
Squamous, omnipotent, and kind;
And under that Almighty Fin
The littlest fish may enter in.
Oh! never fly conceals a hook.
Fish say, in the Eternal Brook,
But more than mundane weeds are there,
And mud, celestially fair;
Fat caterpillars drift around,
And Paradisal grubs are found;
Unfading moths, immortal flies,
And the worm that never dies.
And in that Heaven of all their wish,
There shall be no more land, say fish.

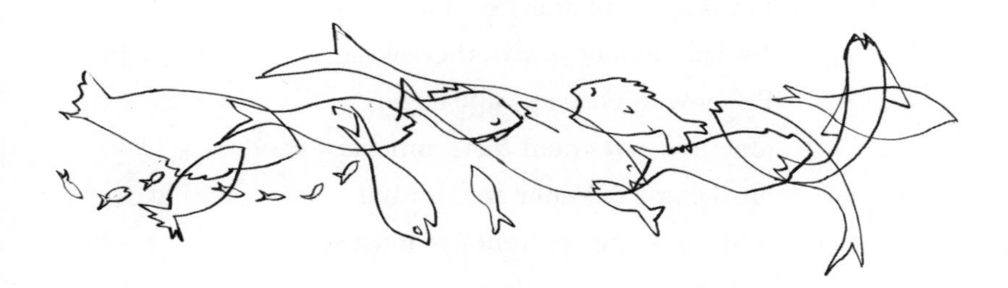

The farmer's wife

Trees Fewster

I always wanted a cat when I was growing up, the youngest of six, in an animal-free household in Amsterdam. I did have one – for about half an hour. I brought it home from a neighbour's and it weed in the corner of a room. My mother sent it back.

I came to London when I was 20 to work as an *au pair* and at the end of the contract came to Yorkshire to work for Dr Barnado's. I'd been so lonely in London that I decided I'd accept every invitation I got so when a friend asked if I'd like to visit his friend who had a farm . . .

It was only seven miles from Leeds, Bradford, Halifax and Huddersfield, in a built-up conurbation in industrial West Yorkshire, yet from the farmhouse we could see only acres and acres of green, undulating land. When I walked into the milking parlour, there was the farmer and that was that. It was love at first sight and we married six months later.

Malcolm was 30 and the 100-acre farm then had a cat, two dogs, geese, cows, pigs, and a few sheep and hens. Very soon we added four children. I knew nothing about farms so I followed Malcolm on the farm walks he did for young schoolchildren. After a few months, I realised he was talking over their heads, assuming they knew things which I knew they didn't, and I took over.

I had to learn everything but it was very interesting. I loved it. And my life. Especially when I thought of my sister back in Amsterdam, living in a flat on the fourth floor, with no lift, a baby and another on the way, and the toilet on the second floor.

Every year, we sell about 20 of our 100 cattle. Every calf is taken from its mother 24 hours after its birth. The mother returns to the herd and the calf goes in a pen with the other calves. Because we're a dairy farm, we can't use male calves, which are either sold at market or, privately, to a beef farmer to be reared for meat. We keep the female calves to replace the dairy cows. I know the cow misses its calf as it spends usually one night crying. That's the way it is, but cows have friends within a herd and that distracts them within a day or two.

My eldest daughter did have a pet cow. She'd talk to it when she was upset and read to it. There came a time when the cow had to be put down and my daughter decided to stand by it as the deed was done. The knackerman was a bit angry but my daughter had felt close to the animal . . . I thought what she did was right.

When the children were young they put a little dead bird into a shoebox and buried it under a 'tree of heaven', sang hymns and took a photograph. Death is part of life, and I'm glad they all learnt that at an early age.

A few months back, on Palm Sunday, a working dog, which belonged to my eldest son, was run over by a tractor. He had a broken leg and his working life was over. The vet couldn't be reached so, while Malcolm and I went to church, my son, who lives next door, came over with his gun. By the time we got home, my son had shot and buried the dog. I was very proud of him. And it reminded me of a time when my children were young. They're all musical and they used to perform in old people's homes. My son used to sing 'Old Shep', a song about a faithful old dog which has had its day, is shot by its owner, a young boy, and goes to heaven.

Malcolm has had a series of terriers over the years. Outside, they're working dogs; inside, they're his lap dogs. He's very fond of them and feeds them titbits at the table. They don't come to me because they know I don't do that. Perhaps I'm a bit harder than my husband. I can pluck a hen and cook it, but he can't.

That said, we had a calf born blind. In a pen, Sandy learnt how to avoid things but when she grew bigger, we knew she'd never survive so she was slaughtered and put in the freezer. We all knew that we were eating Sandy. That's the way it is. The other night, I prepared a whole fish, with its head and tail, and before I put it in the oven, I showed it to my two-year-old granddaughter. She knew what it was, and I think that's the way it should be: that the fish had lived, and was killed in order for us to eat.

It's like the December, many years ago, when my eldest son was late for school, and the teacher wanted to know why. He said he'd had to catch Christmas Day lunch. That's the reality.

A Farmer's Boy

Anon

They strolled down the lane together,
The sky was studded with stars –
They reached the gate in silence
And he lifted down the bars –
She neither smiled nor thanked him
Because she knew not how;
For he was just a farmer's boy
And she was a Jersey Cow.

The vet

Peter Knapp

I've been a vet for more than 30 years, and established Parkside Veterinary Centre more than 20 years ago. My unwritten ethos is: listen to what the owner says, however silly it sounds, because they know their pet best.

At home, aside from my wife and children, I have two dogs, two fish and a hamster. At Parkside we have five vets and ten nurses, providing on-site care seven days a week, with emergency and in-patient facilities which are air-conditioned, and under-cage heating in the stainless-steel kennel block. As well as the more usual domestic animals, the practice sees a lot of local wildlife, via London Wildcare and the public, and in my time, I've treated koi carp, wallabies, racoons, even a panther cub. I operate a global discussion list and website for vets, and discuss cases with colleagues in-house or on the list.

On average, we deal with two to four deaths a day. Some are natural, some trauma or illness, some animals are dead on arrival, some we euthanase, mostly for health reasons, but we do have cases of the biting dog or the incontinent animal where the owner can't or won't cope.

Strong bonds can develop between people and pets and these can end in painful losses, and, yes, there are special ones which get to you – mostly because animals don't judge in the same way as people. Telling people their pet is dying and should be euthanased goes with the job. If it can't be helped, I don't have a problem. It's way, way harder if there is an untoward death or a death from a procedure carrying a low but known risk.

Death is not so desperate if it's due to old age or a progressive disease or nasty illness where we're doing the pet a favour, but it's harder when it's through stupidity – a road accident, a gate left open, or garden toxins. I was more upset when my favourite young cat got run over than when another went into age-related

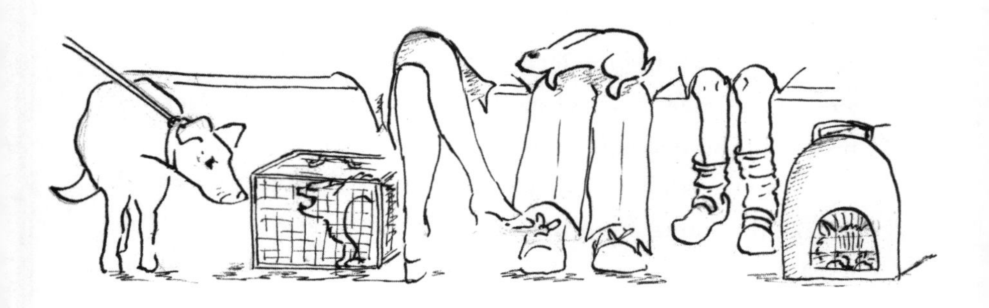

congested heart failure and died while I was trying to help it. Equally, I was upset when I had to euthanase my first dog with a leukaemia that did not respond to radiation/chemotherapy, but it had had lots of happy years and that reconciled me.

I come from the age of 'It's happened, you deal with it', but my nurses are very good at talking to people. We offer options of burials, cremation, and ashes returned in assorted urns or caskets. For myself, I have no wish to keep bits of ash or fur as a memento. Call it a deficiency but, for me, it's the living pet that was the personality not the cadaver.

It's very, very rare for people to refuse permission to euthanase a sick pet and although, legally, we have the right and obligation to euthanase if we see fit, I didn't sign up to drag a pet from an hysterical owner. So, an option would be to load it with massive pain relief so that it's unaware while the owner comes to terms with reality or the animal dies. If an owner were away or uncontactable, we'd seek colleagues' opinions before we took any action. In the last resort, we'd contact a welfare organisation, such as the RSPCA, which has more legal expertise and muscle.

The people who make us groan are those who come in, patently wanting an animal euthanased and, although we can help it, that is not what they want to hear. Whatever the reason behind their intent (money, nuisance, a genuine belief that it's for the best), it seems some folk want us to carry the blame for the decision so that they can feel less guilty. They don't want to hear alternatives, referrals to charities, or treatment options. And this problem is more common than one would wish.

It takes diplomacy, but over the years we have managed to take the animal from the owner, treat it, and rehome it. The most dramatic case was a five-month-old German shepherd pup, which had a broken leg. At least the owner was brutally honest that he wasn't going to look after it and was pleased to go home without paying any bill. The dog was rehoused the same day to a very nice man and happily went home with him in her plaster cast.

Four-Feet

Rudyard Kipling
1865–1936

I have done mostly what most men do,
And pushed it out of my mind;
But I can't forget, if I wanted to,
Four-Feet trotting behind.

Day after day, the whole day through –
Wherever my road inclined –
Four-Feet said, "I am coming with you!"
And trotted along behind.

Now I must go by some other round, –
Which I shall never find –
Somewhere that does not carry the sound
Of Four-Feet trotting behind.

Henrietta, the hen

Annie Rapoport, music student

I'm number three in a family of six children and we've always had pets. My earliest memories are of our cats, Pusky and Whoosky, who I recall were always in the kitchen but that may be because that's where their food was. Tocas, our tortoise, arrived when I was two. Later, we had a mouse and various hamsters including two Russians, Frank and Nordberg (named after the *Naked Gun* characters), who were not very friendly. Russian hamsters are notoriously territorial and don't like being lifted out of their cages.

I got Henrietta for my ninth birthday, with two other hens. Mummy built them a henhouse, with a run, but they were often let loose in the garden. I was very fond of them all but I was instantly mad about Henrietta. I'm not sure why. She did look different from the other two. She had lighter, softer feathers and looked cuddlier, like a teddy bear. She was approachable and sweet, confident and brave, and didn't seem to mind being cuddled. A lot of the hens we've had are difficult to approach and pick up because they're naturally suspicious – even of the people who feed them – and run away from you. Henrietta was friendly with most people. Did she recognise me? I'm not sure.

She was probably between 14 and 18 weeks old, as hens usually are when they're bought from a farm or market. Because they were 'my' hens, for my birthday, I looked after them, although, looking back, Mummy probably did all the hard stuff. But I did feed Henrietta nice bread and potato peelings. Like most hens, she loved potato peelings. And I had a book, given to me by family friends, that taught me about caring for hens.

I remember Odile, my eldest sister, laughing when she found me in the potting shed, talking to Henrietta. But I liked spending time with her, just reading or chatting, when she and the other two hens were loose in the garden.

Once we were all late for school because, as we were about to leave home, we saw the three hens up on the roof of the air-raid shelter next to our house. My sister, Izzy, who was seven, tried to explain this to her teacher but he told her off for lying and sent her to stand in the corner.

One day, when I was 11, I remember going out to the chicken run and finding Henrietta completely still and stiff and, for a few minutes, I couldn't accept that she was dead. I felt terribly sad because she was my pet and, for a hen, she'd lived a long life and I'd got used to her being around. I sat in the run for some time, and then went to tell Mummy that Henrietta was dead, all the time hoping that I was wrong and that really she was still alive.

Henrietta was one of the few of our hens who didn't meet her end in the jaws of the fox, so I know I was lucky she was around as long as she was. Mummy helped me bury her in a corner of our garden, near the pond, where we buried some other pets. I think I marked the spot with some stones.

I don't remember but I'm told that night my parents had a dinner party and I spent the whole evening sitting on the floor sobbing my heart out, with Izzy and a friend of Mummy's sitting beside me, trying to console me. I don't remember many details about my time with Henrietta but I haven't forgotten the feelings – of loving her and of being very upset when she died.

Now that I'm older, I suppose I realise that hens are functional pets, there to provide food. They don't have long lives and it is sad when that life is cut short by a fox, but hens are not like cats, which are with you for years and years and are definitely part of the family.

Hen's Nest

John Clare
1793–1864

Among the orchard weeds, from every search,
Snugly and sure, the old hen's nest is made,
Who cackles every morning from her perch
To tell the servant girl new eggs are laid;
Who lays her washing by, and far and near
Goes seeking all about from day to day,
And stung with nettles tramples everywhere;
But still the cackling pullet lays away.
The boy on Sundays goes the stack to pull
In hopes to find her there, but naught is seen,
And takes his hat and thinks to find it full,
She's laid so long so many might have been.
But naught is found and all is given o'er
Till the young brood come chirping to the door.

Sweep, the cat

Ann Widdecombe, MP for Maidstone and The Weald

We always had animals at home, usually a cat and dog together, except for a period when we lived in Singapore. If I have to choose one to recall from childhood it has to be Monty, a smoky-coloured cat. Monty was affectionate, very intelligent and a great character. We were moving house and put him into an empty room where there was a window with two catches. Somehow, he managed to open both catches and escape. Luckily, we recovered him two days later.

In my adult life, I've had six cats – Sooty, Sweep, Pugwash the First, Carruthers, Pugwash the Second (named because Pugwash the First sadly died young at four years old), and Arbuthnot. I like to give my cats hilarious names. But it has to be Sweep, a black and white, who was my special cat. He came with Sooty, a pure black, and a flat I was buying in Fulham. Somewhat facetiously, I asked the woman who was selling up and moving to Spain whether the black cat came with the property. She said, well, yes, actually, he did. But it took her a few minutes to pluck up the courage to tell me that there was another cat that went with him.

Sweep was very round, very plump, very, very furry and agreeable. He and Sooty were with me before I became an MP and then they became Westminster cats. Sweep went on to become Ministerial. I've got a picture of him sitting on a red box. He particularly liked sleeping on social security papers but he didn't care for prison papers.

They both ate Whiskas during the week but, as this is a Catholic household, they had fish on Friday, which they loved. I'd get raw cod from my local fish and chip shop, and the Greek owners taught me the Greek words for raw fish, which I've now forgotten.

Before I became an MP, I worked regular hours and Sooty and Sweep both knew when I was coming home. Sooty would sit on the window ledge, watching people and cars come and go, and Sweep would be by the front door, sitting on the mat. A friend waiting once in my flat watched them ignore everyone and everything else and then saw how they reacted when my car pulled up.

Sweep outlived Sooty and lived to be 23 years old. I'd been getting a bit nervous about him as he'd suddenly got very thin, and I'd thought this was it. I'd had to go to Scotland for three days, and a friend looked after him. The night before I came home he'd eaten his supper and seemed fine. But when I got back, there he was, close to the mat where he used to wait for me. I knew by his body temperature that he'd only just died.

How did I feel? Obviously, abominable. But there we were in a first-floor flat, with no garden, at the height of summer. I took a taxi to the vet, with Sweep in his carrier. The driver asked if he was poorly and I said, 'No, he's dead.' When the time came for me to pay the fare, he wouldn't take any money.

I had Sweep cremated, like all my pets. And like them all, his ashes are in a box, stored in London. When I retire, I'll bury them all in the garden, perhaps under an apple tree.

Do I believe that my pets will be with me in an after-life? My faith teaches the opposite, that animals have no soul. I'm resigned to it but, occasionally, I do fantasise about Sooty and

Sweep curled up in some celestial armchair, being fed fish by the angels.

So why do I have cats? I love them. They're delightful. They give me huge amounts of amusement, and vet bills. I wouldn't want to be without them; they're a pleasure to have around.

Although I now have a vet who'd come out at any hour of the night, it was not always so and I get very angry about the lack of a comprehensive 24-hour veterinary service. It's partly due to my own experiences over the years. Once, in the middle of the night, when Sweep was about 18, he wouldn't stop yelling and his legs were all wobbly. Our vet's surgery was on answerphone and no vet I phoned would come out except one, but he was too far away. I rang the RSPCA, who weren't interested because it was a domestic animal. Neither the Blue Cross nor the PDSA could help. The same thing happened when I lived in Fulham and saw an Alsation knocked down in the road. A vet told me I'd have to bring the dog to him. I wondered if he'd considered the weight of such a dog, and its mood when it was injured.

It made me very angry and put me off vets for a while because what can you do if your pet is seriously ill, you're an old lady, and it's three o'clock in the morning?

Pugwash the Second and Arbuthnot are now 10 and 11, respectively. With any luck, they will still be around when I retire to Dartmoor. It will be a very contented household. You will find it by the purrs.

La Ménagerie intime

(an extract)

Théophile Gautier
1811–1872

It is no easy task to win the friendship of a cat. He is a philosopher, sedate, tranquil, a creature of habit, a lover of decency and order. He does not bestow his regard lightly, and, though he may consent to be your companion, he will never be your slave. Even in his most affectionate moods he preserves his freedom, and refuses a servile obedience. But once gain his confidence, and he is a friend for life. He shares your hours of work, of solitude, of melancholy. He spends whole evenings on your knee, purring and dozing, content with your silence, and spurning for your sake the society of his kind.

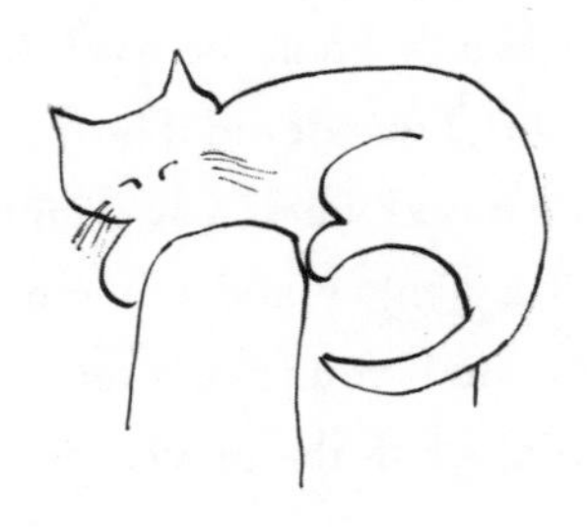

Victor, the dog

Joan Burgess, retired civil servant

Victor was brought to our house by a family friend some time after he was born in July, 1941. We took one look at him and that was it. I was nine and he was given to me, but my mother, older brother and sisters all loved him. We called him Victor as it was a particularly bad time in the war, but he got called Teddy because he looked like a cuddly bear and The Old Puppy because he was always boyish, right to the end.

When Victor was a puppy, I remember seeing my only two pairs of school uniform stockings hanging on the washing line, one with its foot savaged off. I had to go to school with a much-darned leg. But I didn't mind.

Victor had a wonderful disposition, not a bad thought in his head; he'd let you take a bone from his mouth. He had a lot of energy but he was very quiet, he'd sneeze or shake his collar to get your attention. The only time I remember him barking was just before a bomb fell quite close to our house, and he growled only when two workmen came round to mend the ceilings, which had collapsed in the blast.

Victor was one of us. He sat at the dining table on his own chair and shared our meal. He had his own plate and his own bowl (of tea), which went everywhere. At Christmas, as the youngest, I took presents out of the sack for everyone and read out the names, and we all gave Victor presents, as we did on his birthday. He'd be surrounded in wrapping paper, thoroughly enjoying himself.

He was white with black ears, a mongrel, and I think he must have had circus blood because among his tricks was the one in which he'd lie on his back and, with trembling front paws, lift a ball or a bone into the air. To this day, I don't know how he did it.

It was love of the purest kind: we wanted to be with him and he wanted to be with us. If, in the winter, he was settled comfortably by the fire, and we were all elsewhere in the house, we would hear a tiny 'wuff' – i.e. 'I'm too comfortable to move but I'd like somebody to come and sit with me.' Needless to say, we always hurried to oblige.

He survived for a few years after he had a big lump removed but then he started to get asthma attacks, a sign of heart failure. He'd simply worn out. We had him put to sleep just before his sixteenth birthday. My brother took him to the vet on the other side of town in a hired car. Victor loved car and train rides and my brother told us afterwards how much Victor had enjoyed that ride,

looking out, interested in everything. When we all came home at the end of the day, we realised we'd left his dishes on the floor. It made us miss him terribly. Victor had a good life and, although it's 50 years since he died, not a day has gone by when I haven't thought about him. R.I.P., little lamb.

The Dog

(an extract)

Jerome K. Jerome
1859–1927

. . . He is very imprudent a dog is; he never makes it his business to inquire whether you are in the right or the wrong, never asks whether you are rich or poor, silly or wise, sinner or saint. You are his pal. That is enough for him . . .

Rosie, the donkey

Sara Rapoport, teacher and artist

As well as my husband and six children, I look after Billy, the goat; Tocas, a tortoise we've had for 20 years; Oliver, an indoor cat, and Spider, a feral cat; and about 20 hens of various breeds. I didn't grow up in a particularly animal-orientated household but we always had a cat and, during the school holidays, I looked after the school rabbit and her litters. I was besotted with horses and have ridden since early childhood. And for as long as I can remember, I've wanted a field with a donkey and a goat in it, perhaps because when I was growing up, I used to pass by Dylan and Fizz who lived in a paddock not far from where we lived. From a practical point, donkeys keep the grass down and tend to be peaceable around children. They are also inexplicably appealing.

So when I heard there was a donkey for sale . . .

I didn't take to the woman on sight and Rosie was anything but a good specimen, nothing like what I'd been led to expect, but I was carried away by my desire to own a donkey. I returned with a friend who had a horsebox and handed over a cheque. On the way home, my friend echoed my concerns in no uncertain manner. She thought Rosie was older than had been claimed and that she was suffering from Cushing's disease, a pituitary problem afflicting mainly horses, which explained why she had a thick winter coat in July.

When I got home I phoned the woman, expressing my concerns over Rosie's age and health, and she insisted I call the mobile phone number of the man from whom she'd acquired the donkey, who would verify everything she'd said, as he'd used Rosie for donkey rides on the beach.

I phoned the man but still I wasn't happy, so I contacted the Donkey Sanctuary – but on a day when their computer had crashed. I gave up. In a way, I felt Rosie was destined to stay.

She was a very gentle animal, very good-natured when children wanted a ride. She didn't bite or kick. She ambled about, not very interested in people or other animals, solitary but content. I don't for one moment think she'd been abused, more neglected. And perhaps for that reason, I never felt she bonded with me, or anyone, unless she thought we had a carrot for her.

She had a catalogue of physical woes, aside from the thick coat which had to be cropped short and expertly, to prevent lice breeding in it. Then, about three years after she'd come to us, she started to limp. The farrier showed me a pink spot in her hoof, which he diagnosed as a tumour. Both he and the vet advised having her put down. I was upset, but also relieved.

It was March. A beautiful sunny day. The friend who'd come with me to buy her arrived and Rosie looked up, probably expecting a carrot.

A van arrived and a man got out, a gun held behind his back, and walked towards us. Rosie, who'd been grazing in the field, came across quietly, willingly, and for once in many, many months, she wasn't limping. I wondered if I was imagining things.

The man went up to Rosie. He was very nice, very gentle as he talked to her and lifted the gun to her head . . . My friend forced me to turn away, urged me into the house to get the man's money. It was all over by the time I came back, and Rosie's body had been winched into the van. If I read the tone correctly, she hadn't known anything about it. But it's the part I hate: when I feel I'm playing God, deciding some animal's fate.

A gunshot is very loud and when I looked next, Billy the goat and Bonkers the sheep were at the paddock gate, staring over, puzzled, bewildered. They'd never ever stood like that before.

It wasn't like losing an animal you've had for years and which has been part of your family, but I like to think Rosie had as good a life as she could. She lived with Billy and Bonkers, and Gertie, our other goat at the time, in a field with a winter shed, near to the house, with all of us, and she could browse through the orchard or the woods, or join us in the garden. She was well fed, well groomed and very much cared for. And having her live with us has convinced me even more that I want another donkey.

Donkeys, Whales & Hippopotomi

(an extract)

Reverend Jonathan Lumby

This bright morning I rose early to see my two donkeys. My path crossed a pasture wet with dew. The donkeys pushed towards me to drink and to munch carrots. I felt their warm breath. I smelt the sweetness of their coats. I stared into the wells of their eyes. Have you ever looked into a donkey's eye?

Within the brown is a black circle, amazingly large, holding calm depths of mystery. The two beasts rubbed their whiskery muzzles against me. I scratched their ears, and savoured the wonder of their friendship.

Esau, a strong jackass, has lived with me since birth – for 24 years. Ruth is the other donkey. Esau loved her so much that when we moved from Somerset her owner could not bear to part Ruth and Esau. So now I have two donkeys – or they have me.

While we stood in the meadow, a thrush bounced over to see us, the warm wind sounded in the trees, and some birds sang. That's how a day should begin!

You have brought animals here to enjoy similar moments. You respond to the grace of animals. You delight in the beauty, the friendship, the mystery of your dog, your cat, your hamster, your horse, your goat. If not, you wouldn't be here. On any day to rejoice in animals is good; on a Sunday it is particularly wonderful . . .

In these summer months I'm an adjunct to these donkeys of mine. In our villages at every fête they are fêted. Throughout hot afternoons I lead Esau and Ruth whilst youngsters balance on their backs . . . I may ask you to lead the animals while I mop my brow.

But if so, beware. You, who are used to horses will make poor leaders of donkeys. Horsey people shorten the halter-rope. They hold the rope by the beast's mouth. They tug briskly. Some pull the halter itself; they haul the animal's head from side to side. Very undignified! the donkeys think, so they refuse to budge a step. When a donkey says no, it means no.

Here's how to lead a donkey, lengthen the rope and walk well ahead, calmly. Let the donkey decide where to place its feet. Let the donkey choose when to pause and assess. Treat the animal as an equal. Give him responsibility to make up his own mind and *then,* when he is sure that you may not think it your decision but his, as a fellow-being and friend he will accompany you.

I have learnt from my donkeys, they insist on being my equals. 'Does Esau belong to you?' I am asked. 'I suppose so,' I reply, 'and I belong to him.' C. S. Lewis entitled his novel *The Horse and his Boy*. Why not?

Taken from a talk Reverend Lumby gave at an Animal Service
in Norfolk, 1997, and used with his kind permission.

Monty, the snake and George, the cat

Paula Vickers, former science teacher

We didn't keep animals at home but my father instilled in me a love of nature, and when I became a science teacher in a school in the 1970s I wanted to pass on that feeling. My lab became more like a zoo. I had rabbits, tree frogs, locusts, African land snails, a giant millipede and a snake called Monty. I wouldn't have birds because of allergies but, to help a pupil, I did house, temporarily and secretly, a chick which was turning into a cockerel. The caretaker grew suspicious but we managed to save the bird from the family cooking pot and it was rehoused by a kindly, if reluctant, aunt.

Today, health and safety rules wouldn't allow a school to keep such a menagerie but I believe a stimulating environment develops an enquiring mind and teaches children a lot about how to care for living organisms and about the cycle of life. It certainly did in one tough school where I worked. Many pupils from deprived backgrounds achieved top grades in their GCSE science exams.

Ideally, and unless they're endangered, I'd prefer animals to live in their natural environment (so now in our garden, the birds have nest-boxes, the fish are in the pond, and the ladybirds have their boxes), but sometimes it isn't possible. Years ago when I was in my early twenties, a friend bought me a rat snake. It was a gesture done with the best of intentions but by the time I was given him, Monty was over three feet long, mature and set in his live-prey eating habits, however much I tried to wean him off.

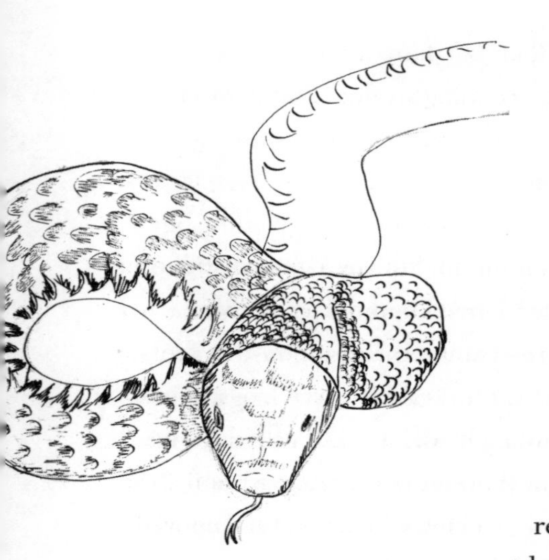

Did Monty have a character? Of course! When I removed the lid of his vivarium, he'd raise his head for me to touch his neck before I lifted him into my arms – unless he was feeling anti-social, in which case he'd just lift up his head and then retire into the box. You don't get love from a reptile, in the way you do from a cat or a dog, but I think he came to recognise the way I handled him and he'd grow twitchy hearing other people's movements across the floor. He mostly had free rein indoors and in all the years I had him, he never once tried to attack me.

You must learn about reptiles before you take one on and try to understand the environment from their perspective. You need to know when they'll defacate, and so leave them in the vivarium; that while they need heat, they must also have a cool area away from a heat mat; that if a lamp is used, it must be kept at a distance so that the animal's skin doesn't burn; that their eyes can't cope with bright sunlight; and that a large bowl of water is necessary for them to bathe in when they're ready to slough off their skin.

I made the mistake of lending Monty to an educational group and someone dropped him. I knew something was wrong when I got him back but the vet couldn't diagnose what it was.

Then, one day after feeding him, I found him dead in his cage with his mouth open and a live mouse running around. I think Monty's injury had left him incapable of asphyxiating the mouse, which had then eaten its way out. I was absolutely horrified. You have to accept it as nature, the revenge of the rodent on the reptile, but I was very, very upset. I buried him in the nearby woods and shed a few tears. I vowed I'd never lend out an animal ever again.

We had a praying mantis, which was an interesting little character. My son was very fond of it and very upset when the crickets ate it while it was shedding its skin and thus was defenceless. And then there was Powerjaws, the hamster . . . But it was different losing George, our beloved cat. We'd just moved house and he escaped through an open window and got out on to the main road. The inevitable happened. I vomited with the shock and could barely talk. Cats and dogs can become really good friends, like family members, but losing them is a loss you have to learn to live with. I tell myself this many times over because I take in old cats from a sanctuary, to give them love and attention in their twilight years.

For a few years, I had my own in-house zoo – with my husband and two growing children. I like to think that I've passed on to our two children a respect for animals, nature and life, and the belief that it's a privilege to care for animals. Also, that at times, when a loved animal dies, for whatever reason, we have to cope with the emotional pain of separation and loss, and an unfounded sense of guilt.

Snake

D. H. Lawrence
1885–1930

A snake came to my water-trough
On a hot, hot day, and I in pyjamas for the heat,
To drink there.

In the deep, strange-scented shade of the great dark carob-tree
I came down the steps with my pitcher
And must wait, must stand and wait, for there he was at the
trough before me.

He reached down from a fissure in the earth-wall in the gloom
And trailed his yellow-brown slackness soft-bellied down, over
the edge of the stone trough
And rested his throat upon the stone bottom,
And where the water had dripped from the tap, in a small
clearness,
He sipped with his straight mouth,
Softly drank through his straight gums, into his slack long body,
Silently.

Someone was before me at my water-trough,
And I, like a second comer, waiting.

He lifted his head from his drinking, as cattle do,
And looked at me vaguely, as drinking cattle do,
And flickered his two-forked tongue from his lips, and mused a
moment,
And stooped and drank a little more,
Being earth-brown, earth-golden from the burning bowels of
the earth
On the day of Sicilian July, with Etna smoking.

The voice of my education said to me
He must be killed,
For in Sicily the black, black snakes are innocent, the gold are
venomous.

And voices in me said, If you were a man
You would take a stick and break him now, and finish him off.

But must I confess how I liked him,
How glad I was he had come like a guest in quiet, to drink at my
water-trough
And depart peaceful, pacified, and thankless,
Into the burning bowels of this earth?

Was it cowardice, that I dared not kill him?
Was it perversity, that I longed to talk to him?
Was it humility, to feel so honoured?
I felt so honoured.

And yet those voices:
If you were not afraid, you would kill him!

. . .

And truly I was afraid, I was most afraid,
But even so, honoured still more
That he should seek my hospitality
From out the dark door of the secret earth.

He drank enough
And lifted his head, dreamily, as one who has drunken,
And flickered his tongue like a forked night on the air, so black,
Seeming to lick his lips,
And looked around like a god, unseeing, into the air,
And slowly turned his head,
And slowly, very slowly, as if thrice adream,
Proceeded to draw his slow length curving round
And climb again the broken bank of my wall-face.

And as he put his head into that dreadful hole,
And as he slowly drew up, snake-easing his shoulders, and
entered farther,
A sort of horror, a sort of protest against his withdrawing into
that horrid black hole,
Deliberately going into the blackness, and slowly drawing
himself after,
Overcame me now his back was turned.

I looked round, I put down my pitcher,
I picked up a clumsy log
And threw it at the water-trough with a clatter.

I think it did not hit him,
But suddenly that part of him that was left behind convulsed in
undignified haste,
Writhed like lightning, and was gone
Into the black hole, the earth-lipped fissure in the wall-front,
At which, in the intense still noon, I stared with fascination.

And immediately I regretted it.
I thought how paltry, how vulgar, what a mean act!
I despised myself and the voices of my accursed human
education.

And I thought of the albatross,
And I wished he would come back, my snake.

For he seemed to me again like a king,
Like a king in exile, uncrowned in the underworld,
Now due to be crowned again.

And so, I missed my chance, with one of the lords
Of life.
And I have something to expiate;
A pettiness.

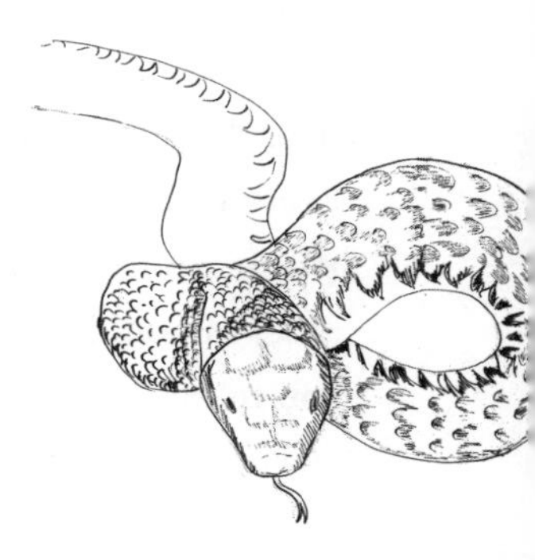

Baby, the goose

Amanda Hill, nurse and holistic therapist

I had a very happy childhood, growing up with my parents, brother and two sisters in a small cottage in Wiltshire set in a four-acre garden. My parents, who were artists (graduates of the Chelsea College of Art), had moved out of London to escape the smog which had aggravated my brother's asthma. We were miles from anyone and anything and, more or less, self-sufficient and self-reliant. We had dogs and kept hens and geese, and had a huge vegetable plot, fruit trees and berry bushes. I was known to be the maternal one, and performed marriage services for our rabbits and guinea pigs, of which we had a good few. But I always wanted a goose of my own.

One day, when I was about 14, my mother, exasperated by the dozens and dozens of unhatched eggs lying about in the geese's pen, collected them all up in a box and then was distracted and left the box on a saddlestone in the garden. I came across it, picked up the eggs one by one and rattled them until I was sure I was holding one that sounded different, as though it had something inside. I popped it into my bra to keep it warm, saying nothing to anyone. I did this every day, and at night I put it in the airing cupboard inside an old nappy. I don't remember exactly how many weeks went by but one day, I heard this tap-tapping noise coming from inside my bra, followed by a loud crack. I couldn't resist taking a peek. I was so excited, I knew I had to be the first thing the goose saw if it was to be mine, and I started helping to peel away the shell.

Minutes later, there it was, soaking wet, looking up at me, and calling out with this lovely little high-pitched voice. It was instant love, of course, on my part. It was so adorable. I dried it off with the gauze lining from a nappy and called it Baby.

Baby lived in my bra during the day and slept beside me in a nappy nest on my pillow. My parents were very nonchalant about it all, seeing it as yet another example of me playing at being mother. I fed Baby grubs from the garden and special grain kept for the other baby birds, and gave him lots of water to drink. He loved water. When he was older he loved me spraying him with the hosepipe and I'm sure there was a time when he had his own paddling pool.

He grew into a fluffy yellow ball, absolutely beautiful, and I took him to school, in my pocket or a satchel. Sometimes he swam about on the fishpond, other times he sat on my lap in class. No teacher objected, and the other children were simply entranced.

Baby grew very quickly, developing great ugly feathers, some of which my father turned into quill pens. It was jolly hard the day I went back to school and had to leave him behind. I remember coming home, walking down the path, and seeing Baby running towards me at high speed, taking off at the last minute, his great wings outstretched. It was a daunting sight, quite scary. At the last moment, he tucked up his feet and folded in his wings and landed gently on my chest. As I supported his body with my arms, he wrapped his long neck round mine, and nibbled and whispered into my ear. It was like a cuddle. And that became Baby's regular welcome home for me.

He knew my voice, and he'd come running and flying to greet me. He was greedy, like most geese, but he had a very nice

nature and was incredibly gentle.

Eventually, my parents decided Baby was too big, and his droppings too large, smelly and copious, to live indoors. So he was given a pen all to himself and he seemed quite happy, living there and escaping from it when he had a mind to. He followed me everywhere and was happy rooting about as I sat nearby, reading a book.

Then my father decided he wanted to reclaim the pen to grow vegetables and Baby, who by now was about three years old, was put into the pen where the other geese lived. I think about it now and realise we wouldn't have done it if we'd known what the consequences would be. One hot day, when all the geese were in the pen, I discovered Baby in the geese's communal shed, lying alone, curled up, dead. There and then, I felt dreadful, very guilty, thinking he'd died of a broken heart, being away from me. Years later, a psychologist friend explained it to me. Baby had never thought himself to be a goose and the other geese hadn't accepted him as one. But I still don't know for sure what really happened.

We buried him in the garden and covered his grave with

flowers. Baby is a big part of my memory of a happy childhood. And I like to think that he is up there, in heaven, with all the animals and people I have liked and loved and would want to see again.

The law arrests . . .

Anon

The law arrests the man or woman
Who steals the goose from off the common;
But lets the greater villain loose
Who steals the common from the goose.

The pet crematorium director

Ray Hale, managing director, Cambridge Pet Crematorium

In the 1970s, when I was working for my uncle, a rag-and-bone merchant, my friend, Clive Jackman, who collected butchers' waste, lost his little Jack Russell. In those days, you took your pet to the RSPCA or the PDSA, or your vet told you to leave it with him and he'd dispose of it. Clive wasn't at all happy; he felt he'd been forced to abandon his pet, had had no time to say goodbye, and was left with a great empty space inside himself. We talked about it, talked some more, and after six months to a year of talk and research came up with the idea of opening a pet crematorium where ordinary, everyday people, like us, could bring their pet for a special or individual cremation.

I remember I was newly married, and I went home one day and told my wife, Lorna, I wanted to remortgage our house to buy a cremator. She just said, 'If that's what you want to do, go ahead, I'm right behind you.'

Today, our 65 members of staff at the Cambridge Pet Crematorium oversee the individual cremation of more than 25,000 pets a year. We have cremation options, a home collection service, a range of caskets and memorials, and we offer counselling. We have a beautiful seven-acre garden of remembrance where owners can scatter their pet's ashes, and on our website there is guidance on bereavement as well as the facility to post a tribute to a pet.

We spent years and years trying to make vets aware of how empty people can feel at the loss of their pet, trying to get them to address the issue of an owner's grief rather than offload it all on to a young, inexperienced veterinary nurse. I used to say to vets: if a doctor told you that your mum was dying, you wouldn't walk off and leave them to dispose of her, would you? So, why should you have to do that to your pet? Now, four times a year, with the Blue Cross Pet Bereavement Service, we hold seminars in different parts of the country, organised as a response to vets asking for training on pet bereavement.

Is all this a bit wimpy? No, I don't think so. Pets play an important part in our lives, perhaps more so in today's society where people can lead a fragmented or quite isolated life. The type of pet is immaterial: we've cremated spiders, elephants, rhinoceroses and giraffes. Whether you're young or old, rich or poor, pets are friends, companions, members of your family. I recall one man sitting in our garden of remembrance, almost inconsolable over the loss of his African parrot which hadn't left his side in more than 30 years. I've seen a distraught middle-aged woman saying goodbye to the horse she had as a 13-year-old schoolgirl.

Do you know, people keep in touch with us over the years, they pop in for a coffee if they're passing. We have thousands of appreciative letters, and we keep them all, which I think shows we're doing something which is right and necessary.

I've heard people say, 'It's only a pet.' I tell them they need to care for an animal to understand what loss means. I remember we had two families in, all upset except for two men, who were smirking, looking as if they didn't know why they were there. A woman in her twenties came in with the ashes of her Border collie and chose a casket which, she was advised, was three times larger than she needed. She explained that she was fulfilling an agreement. A few months before, she'd lost her husband. Before he'd died, she'd promised him she'd scatter his ashes with those of their dog on one of the walks all three had enjoyed together. The casket was for the ashes of her husband as well as her dog. I saw the expressions change on the faces of those two men. Suddenly, they understood what it was all about.

I've had pets all my life and doing this work doesn't make me immune to grief. A big part of my life was my dog, Zak. We all have a special pet. And he was it. A dog in a million. I'd lost Ben, my old German shepherd, and I went to Battersea Dogs and Cats Home to see if I could get another. I looked and looked but

no dog seemed to have quite the right temperament, which was important because at the time we had three very young children. But then I turned round and saw this black German shepherd. They said he wasn't at all suitable, that he was highly nervous, having been beaten up and whipped by a previous owner. I asked to go into his cage and he let me stroke his head. As I walked out of the cage, he followed me. That was it! From then on, he seldom left my side. He came with me to work, and sat at my feet. He might've looked like the sort of dog who'd bite off your head, but many a time he'd nuzzle up to a grieving owner as if to say he was there to help them.

My wife rang me at work one day to say that Zak was ill. I rushed home and took him to the vet. His stomach had ruptured. I waited and went to see him when he was settled in his cage. He tried to get up but couldn't. He didn't make it through the night and when I got the call, I was devastated.

I went through the system at CPC, and, like everyone else, felt this yawning gap inside me. I felt absolutely terrible and cried my eyes out. It's part of the process we all have to go through. And now, when I think of him, when I look at pictures of him, I smile. I have such good memories of him. I was so lucky. He was such a character, such a fantastic dog.

Amazing, isn't it – the impact a few kilos of fur has on you? But I'm no different from anyone else.

The Power of the Dog

Rudyard Kipling
1865–1936

There is sorrow enough in the natural way
From men and women to fill our day;
And when we are certain of sorrow in store,
Why do we always arrange for more?
Brothers and sisters, I bid you beware
Of giving your heart to a dog to tear.

Buy a pup and your money will buy
Love unflinching that cannot lie –
Perfect passion and worship fed
By a kick in the ribs or a pat on the head.
Nevertheless it is hardly fair
To risk your heart for a dog to tear.

When the fourteen years which Nature permits
Are closing in asthma, or tumour, or fits,
And the vet's unspoken prescription runs
To lethal chambers or loaded guns,
Then you will find – it's your own affair, –
But . . . you've given your heart to a dog to tear.

When the body that lived at your single will,
With its whimper of welcome, is stilled (how still!),
When the spirit that answered your every mood
Is gone – wherever it goes – for good,
You will discover how much you care,
And will give your heart to a dog to tear!

We've sorrow enough in the natural way,
When it comes to burying Christian clay.
Our loves are not given, but only lent,
At compound interest of cent per cent,
Though it is not always the case, I believe,
That the longer we've kept 'em, the more do we grieve;
For, when debts are payable, right or wrong,
A short-time loan is as bad as a long –
So why in Heaven (before we are there)
Should we give our hearts to a dog to tear?

The pet bereavement counsellor

Jo-Ann Dono, head, the Pet Bereavement Support Service, and director, SCAS

The Pet Bereavement Support Service is a service set up in 1994 by SCAS (the Society for Companion Animal Studies), after research showed there was no real support for people suffering bereavement at the loss of a pet. It began as a helpline, manned by volunteers, and from the outset grew tremendously. In fact, to such an extent that five years later, and in partnership with The Blue Cross, a lottery grant enabled the service to go national.

We now have a freephone helpline (8.30 am to 8.30 pm every day of the week), manned by co-ordinators who can direct a caller to one of 90 befrienders nationwide. An email service was launched a few years ago which provides another support option for pet owners. *(Please see page 115 for contact details.)*

It takes a lot of courage for someone who has lost their pet to make that first phone call. They can be in huge distress and yet, sometimes, three to five minutes talking to a co-ordinator can be enough. If it isn't, a caller is given the first name, phone number and hours worked by the befriender nearest to them.

Many of our befrienders work full-time, a number in the housing sector or with elderly people; some are at home with children. We try to create opportunities for people with mobility problems or, indeed, whatever someone's circumstance. A befriender must commit to a minimum of six hours a week to take calls in their own home, after completing a correspondence training course over a period of between four and six months.

A befriender is different from a formally trained counsellor who is an 'external' expert. A befriender is a listening ear, offering reassurance that a great sense of loss is normal and understandable, and is not a sign of madness.

The initial contact call to a befriender lasts usually about 40 to 45 minutes and the caller is given the option to call back which they do, on average, two or three times. That said, some people ring back once simply to say thank you, others to say that they've got another pet. Of course, there are people who take six months or longer to heal and there are some you realise will carry their grief for the rest of their life. And, yes, some people's problems aren't solely to do with the loss of their pet – they have their own life issues – and our befrienders have details of other more appropriate organisations which the caller might wish to contact.

People can feel guilty about taking the life of something they love, wondering if they could or should have done things differently. But it's a question of responsibility and quality of life. You are the animal's carer, and the animal is looking to you to do the best you can for it.

The loss of a young animal or an unexpected loss due to something such as a road traffic accident can cause a lot of shock and despair, and self-questioning about whether the death could have been prevented. And for people whose pet has gone missing, coming to terms with a loss when there is no body is also not easy.

Why do we grieve for a lost pet? There are as many different reasons as there are people. Pets tend to be always there, a constant in your life, and when they die, you realise how much you miss them. You sense the gap and raw emotion of loss. And the bond can be a pure, uncomplicated form of affection, of love. Dana, my Labrador, sitting happily at my feet, is nine. I've had her since she was six weeks old and I bring her into work every day. We're inseparable and my family have told me that they don't want to be around me when she goes.

I grew up in a dog-and-cat household, with the occasional hamsters, rabbits and birds, and now I'm a trained psychologist, with experience in counselling, social psychology and academia, but that doesn't stop me grieving when one of my pets dies. But my knowledge helps me understand that it's perfectly normal to feel I've suffered a big loss, and that this awful feeling will come to an end.

I think it helps to be prepared so I'd recommend that an owner recognises that their pet is more likely to die before they do and, with that in mind, they enjoy the time they spend with their pet. As the pet gets older, they should think about its life ending and, if they have the choice, how and where they'd want it done. I'd advise discussing the options with a vet. There are many more choices, including cremation or home burial, than there were 10 to 15 years ago. It can also be helpful to take on a younger animal as your pet gets older. Very often this can give an older pet a new lease of life and it can also help the owner with the grieving process when the older pet dies.

Last year, I lost my cat Pushkin, a part Burmese, after a long struggle with cancer. I was absolutely shattered and then suddenly, months down the line, I decided to take in two Burmese kittens. They're a lot of work, my 'posh' cats, as I call them, but I think of them as a tribute to Pushkin and I'm enjoying the energy and lightness they bring into my home, and I'm enjoying reinvesting my love in two other animals. It's what our befrienders tell every caller: most people recover sufficiently to get another animal. It's not right for everyone, but it was certainly right for me.

If It Should Be

Anon

If it be I grow frail and weak,
And pain should wake me from my sleep,
Then you must do what must be done,
For this last battle can't be won.
You will be sad, I understand,
Don't let your grief then stay your hand,
For this day more than all the rest,
Your love and friendship stand the test.
We've had so many happy years,
What is to come will hold no fears,
You'll not want me to suffer, so,
When the time comes, please let me go.

I know in time you too will see,
It is kindness you do me,
Although my tail its last has waved,
From pain and suffering I've been saved.
Do not grieve that it should be you,
Who has to decide this thing to do
We've been so close, we two, these years,
Don't let your heart hold any tears.

Bob, the dog and Brains, the cat

Susie Cornfield, writer and publisher

I grew up with an Alsatian cross, rescued from Battersea Dogs and Cats Home. I'm an only child and for 10 years Bob was my greatest friend. My mother says that when I was a baby she watched dumbstruck from the top of the house as Bob saw off what she took to be a potential kidnapper creeping up on my pram in the back garden.

When I was a toddler Bob patiently let me dress him in baby clothes and, when measles and chickenpox confined me to a darkened bedroom, he stayed with me throughout a long, tedious summer.

Wherever we went, Bob came too, until family circumstances removed him to live with Auntie Sylvia in Liverpool, hundreds of miles away. It was supposedly a temporary measure but Bob never came home. My mother said he'd settled in too well to be moved again. The last I saw of him, he was staring out of a newspaper, in an advert for the anti-vivisection society which had approached my aunt in the street, asking for a photograph of his wise old, sad old eyes. I missed him but was proud of him, and chuffed that someone else had also seen how special he was.

Years went by, with long working hours and no animals, and then, during a prolonged, mostly horizontal bout of back problems, a friend recommended getting a cat. A cat? No self-respecting dog person has a cat. Besides which, cats'd have your eyes out, soon as look at you. No, no, no . . .

Which is when Brains came into my life.

One vaguely upright evening, two ladies from The Cats' Protection Society arrived with several cages. My friend was there because, although I'd researched the subject of cat-care, I was doubtful. Not to say scared. I was interviewed about my cat-experience and cat-commitment and then the first cage was opened. A tall, skinny, black and white creature strode purposefully across the room towards me, jumped on to my lap and settled there without giving me a second look. I was hooked. And remained so for the 16 years we were together.

Until the end, Brains was at the door to welcome me home, and at the door to follow me if I went out, so, I took to driving round the corner, out of sight, before continuing journeys on foot. She'd wait out in all weathers, complaining vociferously to neighbours who consequently came to know my every movement.

Brains was vocal and I'm sure had perfect pitch. She complained bitterly when I attempted to learn the piano but sat contentedly under the piano stool when a young, accomplished friend came round to play. I took to learning the flute and in the early days, Brains would yowl and tap the end of the instrument, as if trying to get me to stop causing this thing any more pain.

For years, she was hostile to visitors, excepting two – Sara, this book's illustrator, and another confirmed cat-aholic – and would slam out of the cat-flap until they'd left, although she did grow to enjoy keeping a close eye on whatever any workman was up to.

She detested the new kitten, which arrived in the house in her middle age but, outside, she'd defend him from two big bullying cats, putting her own safety at risk. She'd sit with me in the bathroom when I was ill, putting a paw on my hand, and when I went horizontal again for weeks, she lay on the bed, one regular visitor asking if she'd been stuffed.

A kind neighbour who cared for Brains while we were away on holiday held the phone to her ear when I called. Brains' ears pricked up. She recognised my voice and we conversed. What? Yes, of course, I'd left her a map with our journey and itinerary dates, etc., and sent her postcards, but I had to call, didn't I? To put her mind at rest.

Brains would've followed me to the ends of the earth and when she died – two operations having failed to remove a virulent cancer – amidst the guilt (should we have had her put to sleep earlier to prevent the misery she went through?), amidst the shock and wretchedness at losing a companion of many years, I realised that this was the first journey she'd made without me.

Why was she named Brains? Because she was tall, skinny, attractive and, well, different from other cats I'd met, characteristics which, for some reason, reminded me of the American actress, Katharine Hepburn. I knew I didn't want to stand in the street calling out, 'Fish, Katharine Hepburn, come get your fish!', so I thought about what made Miss Hepburn different from many other actresses of her day. It was easy. So, Brains it was.

If Brains were here now she'd be sitting on this desk beside me as I write, as she was beside me in the good times and those times of despair we all endure. I feel immensely privileged to have loved and cared for so singular a creature and, while I have no idea if there is a heaven, I only know that for me, there can't be one if Brains, my MagnifiCat, isn't there beside me. Farewell, my Lovely.

Last Words to a Dumb Friend

Thomas Hardy
1840–1928

Pet was never mourned as you,
Purrer of the spotless hue,
Plumy tail, and wistful gaze,
While you humoured our queer ways,
Or outshrilled your morning call
Up the stairs and through the hall –
Foot suspended in its fall –
While, expectant, you would stand
Arched, to meet the stroking hand,
Till your way you chose to wend
Yonder, to your tragic end.

Never another pet for me!
Let your place all vacant be;
Better blankness day by day
Than companion torn away.
Better bid his memory fade
Better blot each mark he made
Selfishly escape distress
By contrived forgetfulness,
Than preserve his prints to make
Every morn and eve an ache.

From the chair wheron he sat
Sweep his fur, nor wince thereat;
Rake his little pathways out
Mid the bushes roundabout;
Smooth away his talons' mark
From the claw-worn pine-tree bark,
Where he climbed as dusk enbrowned
Waiting us who loitered round.

Strange it is this speechless thing,
Subject to our mastering,
Subject for his life and food
To our gift, and time, and mood;
Timid pensioner of us Powers
His existence ruled by ours
Should by crossing at a breath
Into safe and shielded death,
By the merely taking hence
Of his insignificance –
Loom as largened to the sense,
Shape as part, above man's will
Of the Imperturbable . . .

Prayer for Gentleness to All Creatures

John Galsworthy
1867–1933

To all the humble beasts there be,
To all the birds on land and sea,
Great Spirit, sweet protection give
That free and happy they may live!

And to our hearts the rapture bring
Of love for every living thing;
Make us all one kin, and bless
Our ways with Christ's own gentleness!

Bibliography

The publisher is grateful for permission to reproduce the following extracts:

'The Power of the Dog' and 'Four-Feet', from *Collected Dog Stories* by Rudyard Kipling (Macmillan, 1934). Used by permission of A. P. Watt Ltd, on behalf of The National Trust for Places of Historic Interest or Natural Beauty

Jimmy, The Dog In My Life by Arthur Bryant (Lutterworth Press, 1960), extract used by permission of David Higham Associates Limited

'Dog's Death', from *Collected Poems 1953–1993* by John Updike, copyright © 1993 by John Updike. Used by permission of Alfred A. Knopf, a division of Random House, Inc.

On A Clear Day (Michael O'Mara Books Limited, 1995), extract from his autobiography used by permission of David Blunkett.

The publisher acknowledges and recommends to interested readers these collections and works in which the following poems, sayings and prose were discovered:

'The Dead Sparrow' by William Cartwright in *Come Hither*, Walter de la Mare (Puffin Books, 1957)

'*La Ménagerie intime*', an extract, by Théophile Gautier in *The Enchanted Cat*, John Richard Stephens (Prima Publishing & Communications, California, USA, 1990)

'A Farmer's Boy', Anon; 'Epitaph on a Hare' by William Cowper; 'Baby Tortoise', an extract, by D. H. Lawrence in *Pet Poems*, Robert Fisher (Faber and Faber Ltd, 1989)

'Snake' by D. H. Lawrence (*Contemporary Verse*, Longmans, 1949 and *The Nation's Favourite Animal Poems*, BBC Worldwide Limited, 2001)

'Little Paws', Anon, in *Bless All Thy Creatures, Lord*, Richard Newman (Macmillan Publishing Co Inc., Collier Macmillan Canada, Inc., 1982)

'Prayer for Gentleness to All Creatures' by John Galsworthy; 'Stray Goat' by Elizabeth Montagu; 'The Trap' by E. G. C. Beckwith; 'The Dog' by Jerome K. Jerome; 'Heaven' by Rupert Brooke; 'Prayer

of a Horse' by Maurice Portal; 'An Epitaph' by Lord Byron in *The Neighbours*, Fougasse (The Universities Federation for Animal Welfare, 1954)
'Lonely House', Anon; 'If It Should Be', Anon; 'Requiem for Pluto', Anon; 'If God Had Wanted A Gerbil', Anon; 'Last Words To A Dumb Friend' by Thomas Hardy in *Goodbye, Dear Friend* by Virginia Ironside (Robson Books, 1994)
'Hen's Nest' by John Clare, found on a website and confirmed by the John Clare Society as being in *Bird Poems* (Folio Society, 1980)
'The law arrests . . .', Anon, found on a website.

Useful information – not exhaustive

Battersea Dogs and Cats Home
4 Battersea Park Road, Battersea, London SW8 4AA
Telephone: 0207 622 3626
www.dogshome.org
Battersea has been rescuing lost and unwanted dogs since 1860 and cats since 1883, and is devoted to reuniting animals with their owners or finding them loving, permanent new homes. In 2005, Battersea received 7,000 stray dogs and 2,000 stray cats. It was known as the Battersea Dogs' Home until 2005.

The Blue Cross
Shilton Road, Burford, Oxon OX18 4PF
Telephone: 01993 822651
www.bluecross.org.uk
The Blue Cross, one of the UK's oldest animal welfare charities, has 11 adoption centres, four animal hospitals and two equine centres and provides veterinary care for the pets of people who cannot afford the fees of private vets. *See entry for SCAS for details of bereavement counselling services.*

Cambridge Pet Crematorium
A505 Main Road, Thriplow Heath, nr Royston, Hertfordshire SG8 7RR
Telephone: 01763 207700
www.cpccares.com
Established in 1979, CPC is a family-owned business offering a wide range of pet cremation services to bereaved pet owners.

The Cinnamon Trust
10 Market Square, Hayle, Cornwall TR27 4HE
Telephone: 01736 757900
www.cinnamon.org.uk
Founded in 1985 by Mrs Averil Jarvis, MBE, The Cinnamon Trust is a national charity helping the elderly and terminally ill care for their pets in the short and long term.

London Zoo
Regent's Park, London NW1 4RY
Telephone: 0207 722 3333
www.londonzoo.co.uk
The world's first scientific zoo opened in 1828 and is now part of The Zoological Society of London, a charity devoted to the worldwide conservation of animals and their habitats, and education.

Parkside Veterinary Centre
61 Ruskin Road, Carshalton, Surrey SM5 3DD
Telephone: 0208 395 8222
www.parksidevet.com – for the practice
www.e-vet.com – for veterinarians, animal health professionals and those interested in animal health and welfare
Five vets and ten nurses provide on-site care seven days a week, with emergency and in-patient facilities which are air-conditioned and have underfloor heating in the stainless-steel kennel block.

The Royal Society for the Prevention of Cruelty to Animals (the RSPCA)
Wilberforce Way, Southwater, Horsham, West Sussex RH13 9RS
Telephone: 0870 33 35 999
www.rspca.org.uk
Since 1824, the RSPCA has worked to promote kindness and prevent cruelty to animals. It has 323 uniformed inspectors and 146 animal collection officers in England and Wales, working round the clock to save animals in distress.

Society for Companion Animal Studies
The Blue Cross, Shilton Road, Burford, Oxon OX18 4PF
Telephone: 01993 825597
Support telephone line: 0800 096 6606
Email support: pbssmail@bluecross.org.uk
www.scas.org.uk
SCAS is a UK-based organisation for interested members of the public and professionals interested in the relationship between humans and pets.

Universities Federation for Animal Welfare (UFAW)
The Old School, Brewhouse Hill, Wheathampstead, Hertfordshire AL4 8AN
Telephone: 01582 831818
www.ufaw.org.uk
UFAW is an internationally recognised, independent, scientific and educational animal welfare charity concerned with improving knowledge and understanding of animals' needs in order to promote high standards of welfare for farm, companion, laboratory, captive wild animals and those with which we interact in the wild.

Goodbye, Dear Friend by Virginia Ironside (£6.99, Robson Books, 1994). A book combining practical advice with people's experiences of losing a pet. Sensitive as well as sensible, as one would expect from one of the great agony aunts.

The Neighbours by Fougasse (UFAW, 1954). A delightful animal anthology of poetry and prose, illustrated by the man himself. A treasure to read and a joy to behold. *Out of print but search www.abebooks.co.uk for a second-hand copy.*

Your Special Animal

The following blank pages are here for you to write about your animal, perhaps to include a picture. Feel free to use (or ignore) these ideas which might remind you of special memories:

Animal's name
Breed
Colouring
Physical distinguishing marks
Age
Origin
Habits
Likes
Dislikes
Cause of death/loss
Special memories
Words, songs or music which remind you of your animal

GARRET
BOOKS